Teaching Learning Strategies and Study Skills to Students with Learning Disabilities, Attention Deficit Disorders, or Special Needs

Related Titles

Strategies for Teaching Students with Learning and Behavior Problems, Fifth Edition
Candace S. Bos and Sharon Vaughn
ISBN: 0-205-34195-0

Validated Practices for Teaching Students with Diverse Needs and Abilities
Susan P. Miller
ISBN: 0-205-30628-4

For more information or to purchase a book, please call 1-800-278-3525.

Teaching Learning Strategies and Study Skills to Students with Learning Disabilities, Attention Deficit Disorders, or Special Needs

Third Edition

STEPHEN S. STRICHART
Florida International University

CHARLES T. MANGRUM II
University of Miami–Coral Gables

Allyn and Bacon
Boston   London   Toronto   Sydney   Tokyo   Singapore

Executive editor: Virginia Lanigan
Editorial assistant: Erin K. Liedel
Executive marketing managers: Stephen Smith and Amy Cronin
Cover designer: Jenny Hart
Production coordinator: Pat Torelli Publishing Services
Editorial-production service: Stratford Publishing Services, Inc.
Electronic composition: Stratford Publishing Services, Inc.

Library of Congress Cataloging-in-Publication Data

Strichart, Stephen S.
    Teaching learning strategies and study skills to students with learning disabilities,
attention deficit disorders, or special needs / Stephen S. Strichart, Charles T. Mangrum II.
—3rd ed.
        p.   cm.
    Rev. ed. of: Teaching study skills and strategies to students with learning disabilities,
attention deficit disorders, or special needs. 2nd ed. c1998.
    ISBN 0-205-33513-6
    1. Learning disabled children—Education (Elementary)—United States. 2. Learning
disabled teenagers—Education (Secondary)—United States. 3. Study skills—United States.
4. Special education—United States. I. Mangrum, Charles T. II. Strichart, Stephen S.
Teaching study skills and strategies to students with learning disabilities, attention deficit
disorders, or special needs. III. Title.

LC4704.73 .S77 2002
371.9—dc21

2001033672

Printed in the United States of America

10 9 8 7 6 5 4 3 2   05 04 03

Contents

Introduction

USING THIS BOOK AND THE CD-ROM ASSESSMENT

This book and the accompanying CD-ROM assessment provide a comprehensive program for helping students with learning disabilities (LD), attention deficit disorders (ADD, ADHD), or special needs to develop the learning strategies and study skills important for success in school.

Features of the Book

1. Provides reproducible teaching activities with suggestions for teaching and answer keys.
2. Covers important study skills and strategies.
3. Includes strategies for reading, math, and writing.
4. Incorporates subject-area content into activities.
5. Provides opportunities for practice and application.
6. Provides mastery assessments and reflections for each chapter.
7. Provides easily understood directions.
8. Includes controlled amount of material on a page.
9. Provides controlled readability.
10. Contains controlled vocabulary.

Features of the CD-ROM Assessment

1. Assesses the strategies and skills taught in the book.
2. Can be easily customized to assess any or all of the strategies and skills taught in the book.

3. Can be self-administered by individual students in 15–20 minutes.
4. Provides a diagnostic profile for individualizing instruction.
5. Provides a report with instructional objectives.
6. Provides a narrative report for communicating results to parents.
7. Entire assessment or selected subtests can be administered.
8. Can be used multiple times with the same student to assess progress.
9. Can be used on Win or Mac systems.
10. Can be used on networked systems.

The **Trial CD-ROM Assessment** found at the back of this book can be used five times. **Try the Trial CD-ROM** with five students to learn how together the assessment and book provide a comprehensive strategies and study skills program.

Information about how to order an **Unlimited CD-ROM Assessment** that can be used any number of times with any number of students is found on page 235.

MAKING THE BEST USE OF THE BOOK AND ASSESSMENT

Here is a plan for using the book and assessment together as a comprehensive program:

1. Administer the assessment.
   THIS IS DONE INDIVIDUALLY AND TAKES ABOUT 15–20 MINUTES FOR EACH STUDENT.
2. Use the Diagnostic Profile to identify instructional needs.
   FOR EACH LEARNING STRATEGIES AND STUDY SKILLS AREA, THE PROFILE INDICATES THAT A STUDENT NEEDS INSTRUCTION, REVIEW, OR NO INSTRUCTION.
3. Use the Recommendations and Instructional Objectives Report to pinpoint instruction.
   FOR EACH LEARNING STRATEGIES AND STUDY SKILLS AREA IN WHICH A STUDENT NEEDS INSTRUCTION OR REVIEW, SPECIFIC INSTRUCTIONAL OBJECTIVES ARE PROVIDED.
4. Use the Narrative Report to communicate with parents.
   THIS REPORT PRESENTS THE RESULTS IN A SIMPLE-TO-UNDERSTAND FORMAT THAT CAN BE SENT HOME TO PARENTS.
5. Use the teaching activities to provide instruction.
   USE THE CHAPTERS IN THE BOOK THAT CORRESPOND TO THE AREAS IN WHICH A STUDENT NEEDS INSTRUCTION OR REVIEW.
6. Group students by instructional needs they have in common.
   STUDENTS WHO NEED INSTRUCTION OR REVIEW IN THE SAME AREAS CAN BE GROUPED TOGETHER.

7. Readminister the assessment to determine progress.
   READMINISTER THOSE SECTIONS OF THE ASSESSMENT
   THAT CORRESPOND TO THE AREAS IN WHICH YOU PRO-
   VIDED INSTRUCTION OR REVIEW.

LEARNING STRATEGIES AND STUDY SKILLS TAUGHT AND ASSESSED

Remembering Information

Learning something is of little value if what is learned cannot be recalled
whenever necessary. In this chapter, students are taught techniques they
can use to retain the important information and ideas they learn from their
teachers and textual materials.

Reading and Taking Notes from Textbooks

Much of the information students must learn in school is contained in their
textbooks. Students must be taught how to obtain information from their
textbooks effectively and efficiently. To do so, students must have a textbook reading and notetaking strategy. In this chapter, students are taught
to use a textbook reading and notetaking strategy called SQRW.

Interpreting Graphic Aids

Students must be taught how to interpret maps, graphs, diagrams, tables,
and charts to increase their understanding of information found in textual
materials. In this chapter, students are taught strategies for interpreting
these graphic aids.

Taking Notes in Class

Students must write in their notes the important information presented by
their teachers. In this chapter, students are taught a strategy for taking class
notes.

Making Good Use of Study Time and Space

Students must make effective use of their time to complete school assignments and prepare adequately for tests. Students also need good
study habits to get good grades. They must also have a good place to study.
In this chapter, students are taught strategies for scheduling their time,
evaluating and improving their study habits, and organizing their study
space.

Preparing for and Taking Tests

Students must demonstrate mastery of information by taking tests given in different formats. In this chapter, students are taught a five-day strategy for preparing for tests. They are also taught how to do well on the following types of tests: multiple choice, true/false, matching, completion, and essay.

Using Reference Sources

Students must be made aware of the many reference sources they can use to achieve success in school. In this chapter, students are taught strategies for using both print and electronic forms of these reference sources: dictionary, encyclopedia, thesaurus, almanac, and atlas.

Writing a Research Paper

Students must be able to do library research and write a research paper. They must be taught to obtain, document, and organize print and electronic information and present it in a clear, written form. In this chapter, students are taught a strategic series of steps to follow when writing a research paper.

Pronouncing Big Words

Having a strategy helps students pronounce the big words they encounter as they read increasingly more complex material. In this chapter, students are taught the P2SWA strategy for decoding and pronouncing big words.

Finding Main Ideas

Students need to know how to determine the main idea as they read paragraphs and selections. In this chapter, students are taught the READ strategy for identifying main ideas.

Learning Word Meaning

Having a strategy helps students learn the meaning of unfamiliar words they encounter as they read a variety of material. In this chapter, students are taught the ACED strategy for learning the meaning of unfamiliar words.

Spelling New Words

Having a strategy helps students learn to spell new words they encounter in their reading and writing activities. In this chapter, students are taught the SCVCR strategy for learning to spell words.

TEACHING NOTES

Here are some things to do when using this book:

1. Go beyond the reproducible activities to provide your students with additional practice in the use of the strategies. It is additional practice with materials that are directly related to classroom objectives that will enable students to achieve greater success in school.

2. Have the students use a study strategy under your supervision until they have mastered it. Students have achieved mastery when they can automatically recall and apply a strategy. Until they have achieved this automaticity, there is no mastery.

3. Share the strategies with colleagues who also teach your students, and encourage your colleagues to have the students use the strategies in their classes as well. This will help to ensure that students generalize and maintain their use of the strategies.

4. Although the various study strategies are presented individually in this book, in reality students will need to use a combination of strategies to complete most assignments. For example, students studying for a test should use strategies for remembering information, reading textbooks, and managing time in addition to test-taking strategies. Use every opportunity to demonstrate or explain to your students how to combine the use of the various strategies presented in this book.

5. Motivate your students to want to use the study strategies taught in this book. We recommend you use the PARS motivation strategy. This strategy has four components: Purpose, Attitude, Results, Success.

   - *Purpose.* Students are more likely to want to learn a study strategy when they understand how the strategy can help them succeed in school. Be sure to explain how its use can help them acquire more information and get better grades in your class and in their other classes.

   - *Attitude.* Your attitude is infectious. If you are enthusiastic about a study strategy, your enthusiasm will transfer to your students, who are then likely to model your positive attitude toward the use of the strategy.

- *Results.* It is important to give students feedback on how well they are applying a strategy. The feedback needs to be very specific so that students understand what they did correctly and what they did wrong. Students need specific feedback in order to know what to do to improve their use of each strategy.
- *Success.* It is important that students experience success in the application of a strategy. Nothing elicits recurrent behavior as well as success.

6. Have students work cooperatively in pairs or small groups to practice applying the strategies to class assignments. Students can take turns demonstrating how a strategy is used or providing feedback on the effectiveness of its use.

Acknowledgments

We express our appreciation to our colleagues at the University of Miami and Florida International University who graciously gave their time to review the activities in this book. Their reactions and recommendations were of great assistance to us. We also wish to acknowledge our university students, many of whom are teachers of students with LD, ADD, or special needs. Feedback from their use of the activities in their mainstreamed, inclusive, and special-education classrooms was extremely helpful to us. In addition, we would like to thank Oma-Gail Simmons of Frostburg State University, Joan Hoffman of Saint Joseph College, and MaryAnn Byrnes of the University of Massachusetts–Boston for reviewing this edition.

Special appreciation goes to Pat Hawthorne, Assistant Librarian for Administrative Services, University of Miami. Pat's assistance was invaluable in the preparation of Chapter Seven, "Using Reference Sources."

Special appreciation also goes to Mykel Billups, a doctoral student in exceptional student education at the University of Miami. Mykel's critical comments were invaluable in the preparation of the book.

About the Authors

Stephen S. Strichart is professor of special education and learning disabilities at Florida International University, Miami, Florida. He graduated from City College of New York and taught children with various types of disabilities before entering graduate school. Dr. Strichart earned a Ph.D. from Yeshiva University in 1972. Since 1975 he has been on the faculty at Florida International University, where he trains teachers and psychologists to work with exceptional students. Dr. Strichart is the author of many books and articles on topics related to special education and study skills.

Charles T. Mangrum II is professor of special education and reading at the University of Miami, Coral Gables, Florida. He graduated from Northern Michigan University and taught elementary and secondary school before entering graduate school. He earned an Ed.D. from Indiana University in 1968. Since 1968 he has been on the faculty at the University of Miami, where he trains teachers who teach students with reading and learning disabilities. Dr. Mangrum is the author of many books, instructional programs, and articles on topics related to reading and study skills.

## CHAPTER ONE

Remembering Information

TITLES OF REPRODUCIBLE ACTIVITIES

USING THE REPRODUCIBLE ACTIVITIES

After you have distributed a reproducible activity, here are suggestions for its use. Define any terms and clarify any concepts students do not know. Feel free to add further information, illustrations, or examples. Wherever possible, relate the activity to actual subject-area assignments.

1-1 Techniques for Remembering Information

Discuss the importance of remembering information. Have students write a statement describing what they do to remember information. Have students read about the techniques for remembering information they will learn to use in this chapter. Then have students complete the activity. Examine the techniques students identify as those about which they need to learn more. Use this information to guide you as you select the reproducible activities most appropriate to use with your students.

1-2 Repetition

Repetition involves reading, writing, and saying information a number of times to remember it. Use the first part of the activity to demonstrate how to use repetition. Then have students fill in the blanks to show what to do when using repetition. Then have students complete the practice activity. Finally, have students write facts they can remember using the repetition technique.

1-3 Mind Picture

A mind picture is a mental image or picture created in the mind, which later can be used to recall information. The picture serves as a place to collect and hold together facts to be remembered. By including names, dates, and places in their pictures, students can remember a substantial set of information.

Introduce the mind picture technique. Have students place the letters MP (for *mind picture*) in front of the sets of information that are appropriately remembered using a mind picture. Finally, have students reflect and write facts they can remember using the technique.

1-4 Grouping

Grouping is a good way to remember things that go together. For example, a list of ten items is easier to remember if the items can be grouped into two or three sets. Introduce the grouping technique. Have students complete the activity.

1-5 Rhyme

Rhyme is the use of verse to remember information. Use familiar rhymes such as the following to demonstrate to students how rhyme is used to remember information.

> In fourteen hundred ninety-two
> Columbus sailed the ocean blue.

Thirty days has September,
April, June, and November.

Use the first part of the activity to demonstrate how to use rhyme to remember information. Then have students complete the practice activity.

1-6 Acronym

Acronyms are formed using the first letter of each fact to be remembered. The letters are arranged to form a pronounceable "word." The acronym may be either a real word or a nonsense word. When an acronym cannot be formed, tell students to form an abbreviation instead.

Review the acronym technique. Demonstrate how acronyms can be either real or nonsense words. Have students complete the activity.

1-7 Abbreviation

Abbreviations are also formed using the first letter of each fact to be remembered. Abbreviations should be used when the letters do not form a pronounceable word. When the facts can be remembered in any order, the letters of the abbreviation can be in whatever order is easiest for students to remember. Sometimes abbreviations have to be formed in a certain order to correspond to the order in which the facts need to be remembered. Introduce the abbreviation technique.

Review the abbreviation technique. Have students complete the activity for abbreviations first in any order and then using a certain order.

1-8 Acronymic Sentence

When using this remembering technique, students create sentences made of words that begin with the initial letter of each of the facts to be remembered. A common example used to remember the order of the planets in our solar system is the acronymic sentence: *My* (Mercury) *very* (Venus) *earthy* (Earth) *mother* (Mars) *just* (Jupiter) *served* (Saturn) *us* (Uranus) *nine* (Neptune) *pizzas* (Pluto). Tell students that acronymic sentences are useful to remember information for which it is difficult to form an acronym or for which an abbreviation would be too long to be remembered.

Review the acronymic sentence technique. Use the Great Lakes seaport example in the first part of the activity to show students how to form an acronymic sentence. Then have students complete the activity.

1-9 Graphic Organizer

Graphic organizers are useful to remember information that is organized by topics, subtopics, and details. A graphic organizer is a visual representation of the information to be remembered.

Review the graphic organizer strategy. Use the example for food groups to demonstrate the use of a graphic organizer. Have students create a graphic organizer using the information provided. Finally, have students create a graphic organizer for the information provided about physical fitness.

1-10 The Remembering Strategy

When students select the appropriate techniques for the demands of a given assignment, they have used a remembering strategy. Have students complete the activity.

1-11 Mastery Assessment and Reflection

Have students complete this assessment when you believe they have learned to use the remembering techniques presented in this chapter. Review the results of the assessment with students. Provide additional instruction as needed.

Think about what you do to remember information for classes, tests, or in your day-to-day activities. Then write a statement that explains what you do.

_____

_____

_____

_____

_____

_____

_____

Here are the remembering techniques taught in this chapter. Read to learn about each. Place a check (✔) in front of each one you included in your statement.

Repetition is a technique in which you read, write, and recite information.

Mind picture is a technique in which you form one or more pictures in your mind.

Categorization is a technique in which you place information to be remembered into categories.

Rhyme is a technique in which you create lines of verse.

Abbreviation is a technique in which you use the first letter of words to form an abbreviation.

Acronym is a technique in which you use the first letter of words to form a new word.

Acronymic sentence is a technique in which you use the first letter of words to create a sentence.

Graphic organizer is a technique in which you visually show how facts are related or organized.

Write the names of the techniques about which you need to learn more.

_____

_____

_____

_____

_____

Repetition

Repetition   is a technique for remembering facts in which you read, write, and say the facts a number of times.

Use repetition   when you want to remember a few facts, usually not more than four or five facts.

How to use repetition
  1. **Read** the facts.
  2. **Write** the facts.
  3. **Say** the facts.
  4. **Repeat** the steps three or more times.

Fill in the blanks to show what to do when using the repetition technique.

First, (1) _____ the facts. Second, (2) _____ the facts.

Third, (3) _____ the facts. Finally, (4) _____ the steps

three or more times.

Practice   Using the repetition technique, try to remember the following underlined facts. When you are through, whisper the facts in another student's ear.

An <u>explorer</u> named <u>Columbus</u> is said to have <u>discovered America</u> in the year <u>1492</u>.

Here are some more facts with which to practice.

- Marco Polo explored Asia and traveled to China in the late 1200s.
- Ferdinand Magellan is famous for sailing around the world in the early 1500s.

On your own   Write facts you can remember using the repetition technique.

_____

_____

_____

_____

_____

_____

_____

6

Mind picture   is a technique for remembering facts by forming one or more pictures in your mind.

Use mind picture   when you can easily form one or more pictures in your mind to help you remember facts.

How to use mind picture
1. **Say** the facts.
2. **Create** one or more pictures in your mind to show all the facts.
3. **Focus** on the picture(s) and say the facts.
4. **Recall** the picture(s) when you need to remember the facts.

Write the letters MP in front of each of the following that would be easy for you to remember using the mind picture technique.

_____ **1.** The years 1914, 1940, 1953, 1986

_____ **2.** Something you saw on TV

_____ **3.** The most interesting thing you did yesterday

_____ **4.** Major wars: World War I, World War II, Korean War, Vietnam War

_____ **5.** The names of the last five presidents of the United States

_____ **6.** The events that took place in the last story you read

_____ **7.** The floats or bands you saw in a parade

_____ **8.** What you ate for your last meal

Practice   Ask a friend to tell you five fun things to do after school. Write the five things here and use the mind picture technique to remember them.

_____

_____

_____

On your own   Write facts you can remember using the mind picture technique.

_____

_____

_____

Grouping

Grouping is a technique for remembering facts that go together in some way.

Use grouping when you need to remember facts that can be placed in groups or categories.

> How to use grouping
> 1. **Look** for ways that facts to be remembered can be grouped together.
> 2. **Write** a name for each group.
> 3. **Write** the facts that go with each group.

Practice Look for ways the following facts can be grouped together. Write a name for each group. Then write the facts under the name of each group.

1. pencil, paper, magazine, pen, book, chalk, chalkboard, poem, cardboard, newspaper

_____

_____

_____

_____

2. field goal, bat, dribble, home run, shoot, touchdown, free throw, fumble, tackle, basket, third base, pitcher

_____

_____

_____

_____

On your own Write facts you can remember using the grouping technique.

_____

_____

_____

_____

Rhyme   is a technique for remembering facts by forming rhymes.

Use rhyme   when the facts you want to remember have words that sound alike.

> How to use rhyme
>   1. **Write** a line that ends with a word to be remembered.
>   2. **Write** a second line that ends with a word that rhymes with the word to be remembered.
>   3. **Repeat** steps 1 and 2 for other words to be remembered.

Here is a rhyme to remember the names Harry and Mary.

> My friend's name is Harry.
> His sister's name is Mary.

Here is a rhyme to remember these names as well as other important facts.

> My friend's name is Harry.
> His sister's name is Mary.
> We are going to their party.
> They live on Harty.

Practice   Fill in the missing words to complete the rhyme that will help you remember that Columbus was a sailor who discovered America in 1492.

> Christopher Columbus was not a tailor.
> 1. He was a good old _____ .
> He sailed across the ocean blue
> 2. and discovered America in the year _____ .

Write a rhyme that will help you remember these facts:

  3. William Shakespeare was a very bright English fellow who wrote a play with the title *King Lear*. He also wrote a play with the title *Othello*.

_____

_____

On your own   Write facts you can remember using the rhyme technique.

_____

Acronym is a technique for remembering facts by forming a word using the first letter of each fact to be remembered.

Use acronym when you want to remember facts whose first letters can be arranged to form a real word or a nonsense word that can be pronounced.

How to use acronym
  1. **Write** the facts.
  2. **Underline** the first letter of each fact.
  3. **Arrange** the underlined letters to form a real word or a nonsense word that can be pronounced.

CALF is an acronym that is a real word. It can be used to remember the names of these states: Arizona, California, Florida, Louisiana.

LEAT is an acronym that is a nonsense word that can be pronounced. It can be used to remember the names of these U.S. presidents: Adams, Eisenhower, Lincoln, Truman.

Practice Form an acronym for each of the following sets of facts.

1. *States:* Delaware, Indiana, Michigan, Nevada

   _____

2. *Birds:* finch, owl, lark, wren

   _____

3. *American cities:* Chicago, Raleigh, Tacoma, Oakland

   _____

4. *Trees:* pine, oak, redwood, birch

   _____

5. *Fruits and vegetables:* apple, tomato, lettuce, endive

   _____

6. *Water life:* bass, carp, salmon, eel

   _____

On your own Write facts you can remember using the acronym technique.

_____

_____

Abbreviation

Abbreviation is a technique for remembering facts using the first letter of each fact you want to remember.

Use abbreviation when you cannot form a word that can be pronounced using the first letter of each fact.

> How to use abbreviation
>   1. **Write** the facts.
>   2. **Underline** the first letter of each fact.
>   3. **Form** an abbreviation using the underlined letters.

Practice Use the abbreviation technique to remember the following facts. These facts can be remembered in any order, so you can arrange the first letters of the facts to form an abbreviation that is easiest for you to remember.

1. *Body parts:* nose, lungs, heart, kidneys

   _____

2. *Animals:* turkey, goose, lion, seal, deer

   _____

3. *Countries:* Canada, Germany, France, Turkey

   _____

Sometimes facts have to be remembered in a certain order. For example, here are three states in order of highest to lowest population: California, Pennsylvania, Delaware. To remember these states in this order, you must use the abbreviation: CPD.

Each of the following must be remembered in order. Write the abbreviation.

4. Money in increasing order of value: penny, nickel, dime, quarter, dollar

   _____

5. Planets in order from outer space to the Sun: Pluto, Neptune, Saturn, Jupiter, Mars

   _____

On your own Write facts you can remember using the abbreviation technique.

_____

_____

Acronymic Sentence

Acronymic sentence is a technique for remembering facts by creating a sentence from words whose first letters help you remember the facts.

Use acronymic sentence when you need to remember a number of facts that are difficult to remember using the acronym or abbreviation techniques.

How to use acronymic sentence
1. **Write** the facts.
2. **Underline** the first letter of each fact.
3. **Create** and **write** a sentence using words that begin with the underlined letters.

The following acronymic sentence was created to remember that <u>M</u>innesota, <u>W</u>isconsin, <u>I</u>llinois, <u>I</u>ndiana, <u>O</u>hio, and <u>M</u>ichigan all have a seaport on one of the Great Lakes.

Indians were mining ore in May.

Practice Use the acronymic sentence technique to remember the facts for each of the following food groups.

1. *Meat group:* steak, liver, veal, pork, chicken

   _____

2. *Dairy group:* milk, egg, cheese, cream, butter

   _____

3. *Fruit and vegetable group:* apple, pear, orange, banana, carrot, bean, radish

   _____

4. *Bread and cereal group:* cracker, rice, pasta, granola, muffin, bun, waffle, pancake

   _____

On your own Write facts you can remember using the acronymic sentence technique.

_____

_____

_____

_____

Graphic organizer is a visual technique for remembering information that contains a topic, sub-topics, and details.

Use graphic organizer when you want to show how a topic, subtopics, and details go together.

> How to use graphic organizer
> 1. **Write** the topic for the information you need to remember.
> 2. **Write** the subtopics for the topic.
> 3. **Write** the details for each subtopic.
> 4. **Draw** a graphic organizer that shows how the topic, subtopics, and details are related.

Look at the following topic, subtopics, and details.

Topic: Food Groups

Subtopics	and	Details
Meat group		steak, pork
Dairy group		milk, cheese
Fruit and		apple, pear
vegetable group		carrot, radish
Bread and		cracker, muffin
cereal group		rice, granola

Study the graphic organizer that shows how the topic, subtopics, and details go together.

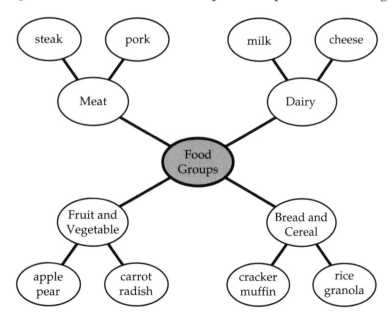

Practice   Create a graphic organizer to remember the following information.

Topic: Physical Fitness

Subtopics	*and*	*Details*
Agility		speed in changing direction
		speed in changing body position
Balance		keeping stable body position
		not falling over
Flexibility		range of motion in a joint
Endurance		continuing activity
		long time period

On your own   Write facts you can remember using the graphic organizer technique.

_____

_____

_____

_____

You have learned eight techniques for remembering information. You must decide which technique to use with a given set of facts. When you make this decision, you are using a remembering strategy.

For each of the following write the name of the remembering technique that would be most appropriate to use to remember the facts.

1. Facts easy to visualize

_____

_____

2. Facts whose first letters can be used to remember the facts

_____

_____

3. A short list of facts you can remember quickly and easily

_____

_____

4. Facts with words that sound alike

_____

_____

5. Topics, subtopics, and details that can be arranged visually to show their relationships

_____

_____

6. Facts whose first letters can be arranged to form a pronounceable word

_____

_____

7. Facts that can be organized into categories

_____

_____

8. Facts that can be remembered by creating a sentence from words whose first letters help you remember the facts

_____

_____

For each of the following, write the name of the remembering technique that was used.

1. Billy created lines of verse that ended with words that sounded alike.

   _____

   _____

2. Rosa organized a set of facts into categories.

   _____

   _____

3. Tony arranged topics, subtopics, and details into a visual display.

   _____

   _____

4. Susie created a sentence from the first letters of facts.

   _____

   _____

5. Luis formed images in his mind.

   _____

   _____

6. Elizabeth wrote and repeated facts several times.

   _____

   _____

7. George remembered in order the first letter of a series of facts.

   _____

   _____

8. Mary used the first letters of facts to create a nonsense word she could pronounce.

   _____

   _____

Reflection How has the remembering strategy made you a better student?

_____

ANSWER KEY FOR CHAPTER ONE

1-1 Responses will vary.

1-2 1. Read.　2. Write.　3. Say.　4. Repeat.

1-3 Students should write MP in front of 2, 3, 6–8.

1-4 1. Things to Write with: pencil, pen, chalk
　　Things to Write on: paper, chalkboard, cardboard
　　Things to Read: magazine, book, poem, newspaper
　2. Basketball: dribble, shoot, free throw, basket
　　Football: field goal, touchdown, fumble, tackle
　　Baseball: bat, home run, third base, pitcher

1-5 1. sailor.　2. 1492.　3. Responses will vary.

1-6 Possible answers.　1. mind.　2. fowl.　3. cort.　4. prob.　5. tale, late.　6. sceb.

1-7 1–3. Responses will vary.　4. pndqd.　5. PNSJM.

1-8 Responses will vary.

1-9

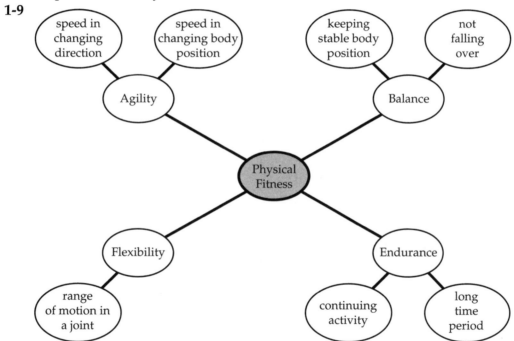

1-10 1. mind pictures.　2. abbreviation.　3. repetition.　4. rhyme.　5. graphic organizer.
　　6. acronym.　7. grouping.　8. acronymic sentence.

1-11 1. rhyme.　2. grouping.　3. graphic organizer.　4. acronymic sentence.
　　5. mind picture.　6. repetition.　7. abbreviation.　8. acronym.

Reflection Responses will vary but should reveal insights into how the student has become
　　a better learner.

## CHAPTER TWO

Reading and Taking Notes from Textbooks

TITLES OF REPRODUCIBLE ACTIVITIES

USING THE REPRODUCIBLE ACTIVITIES

After you have distributed a reproducible activity, here are suggestions for its use. Define any terms and clarify any concepts students do not know. Feel free to add further information, illustrations, or examples. Wherever possible, relate the activity to actual subject-area assignments.

2-1 Learning about SQRW

Tell students that the formula SQRW stands for the four steps of a strategy for reading and taking notes from textbooks. Use the information in the activity to explain what students are to do for each step of the SQRW strategy. Have students underline the key words that will help them remember what to do for each step.

2-2 Learning How to Use SQRW

Have students read about how a student named Mary completed the Survey (S) step of SQRW for her reading assignment, "Earth." Elaborate on what Mary did and answer any questions. Repeat this procedure for the remaining three steps.

2-3 Applying SQRW to a Social Studies Reading Assignment

Have students apply what they have learned about SQRW to the social studies reading selection titled "Money." Have students complete the Question–Answer Notetaking Form. Students may need more than one copy of the form to write their questions and answers. Two questions and answers are provided as models.

2-4 Applying SQRW to a Science Reading Assignment

Have students apply what they have learned about SQRW to the science reading selection titled "Amphibians." Have students complete the Question–Answer Notetaking Form. Tell students they now know how to use SQRW to read and take notes from assignments in their subject-area textbooks.

2-5 Mastery Assessment and Reflection

Have students complete this assessment when you believe they have learned to use SQRW. Review the results of the assessment with the students. Provide additional instruction as necessary.

SQRW is a strategy for reading and taking notes from textbooks. Each letter in SQRW stands for a step in the strategy. Use this rhyme to remember the steps:

Survey, Question, Read, and Write
That will make your notes just right

Here are the four steps in SQRW. As you learn about each step, underline the words that will help you remember what to do for that step.

<u>S</u>urvey   In this step you read to learn what a textbook chapter is about. You read the:

✔ *Title.* It is found at the beginning of the chapter. The title tells the general topic of the chapter.
✔ *Introduction.* The introduction gives an overview of the information in the chapter. It is found in the first paragraph or two of the chapter.
✔ *Headings.* The headings tell the specific topics that will be covered in the chapter.
✔ *Summary or Conclusion.* A summary restates the main points made in the chapter. A conclusion provides a generalization made from the facts and ideas presented in the chapter. A summary or a conclusion is usually found in the last paragraph or two in the chapter.

<u>Q</u>uestion   In this step you form questions that help you understand what to look for as you read. You:

✔ Use the words *who, what, where, when, why,* or *how* to change headings into questions. Sometimes more than one question needs to be created for a heading.
✔ Write the question(s) on the Question–Answer Notetaking Form. Your teacher may ask you these questions in class or on a test.

<u>R</u>ead   In this step you read to find the answers to your questions.

<u>W</u>rite   In this step you write your answers on the Question–Answer Notetaking Form.

In the next activity you will learn how a student used SQRW to read a chapter in a textbook.

Read to learn how a student named Mary used SQRW to read a textbook chapter titled "Earth," found on pages 22–24. The parts of the chapter are labeled to help you follow what Mary did. The Question–Answer Notetaking Form completed by Mary is found on page 25.

S reminded Mary that the first step was to begin with a **survey** of the chapter. Why? Because she wanted to know the general topic of the chapter before she began reading. She began her survey by reading the *title*. She learned that the chapter was about the planet on which we live because the title was "Earth."

Next Mary read the *introduction*. This is what she learned:

> Earth is one of nine planets that revolve around the Sun.
> Earth is the third-closest planet to the Sun.
> Earth is the right distance from the Sun to support life.

Next Mary read each *heading*. By reading the headings, she learned that the specific topics covered were the shape, mass or weight, layers, core, atmosphere, and changes on the planet Earth.

Finally Mary read the *summary*. This gave her a review of the main points in the chapter.

Q reminded Mary to form **questions** from headings using the words *who, what, where, when, why,* or *how*. She formed questions to know what to look for as she read. Mary changed the first heading, *Shape*, into the question, "What is the shape of Earth?"

R reminded Mary to **read** to find the answer to her question. She learned that the answer was "round." As Mary continued to read, she found that the information under the heading *Shape* also told how Earth got its shape. So she formed another question, "What determined the shape of Earth?" Mary found the answer was, "gravity and centrifugal force." She now had two questions and answers for the first heading.

W reminded Mary to **write** her questions and answers on the Question–Answer Notetaking Form. This gave her a written record of her questions and answers.

Mary repeated the QRW steps for each heading until she finished reading the chapter.

Look at the reading selection from a textbook as your teacher explains how to use SQRW.

Earth

Earth is just one of nine planets that revolve around the sun. These planets and the Sun form our solar system. Earth is the third-closest planet to the Sun. It is at the right distance from the Sun for the evolution of life as we know it.

SHAPE

Although Earth appears to be perfectly round in shape, it is not. It is shaped like a ball, but not perfectly. Earth is flatter at the poles than at the equator. The distance around Earth through the north and south poles is approximately 27 miles less than the distance around Earth at the equator. Yet when seen in a photograph from outer space, Earth looks perfectly round. Because of its tremendous size, the bulges at the equator and dips at the poles are not noticed.

The shape of Earth is determined by both gravity and centrifugal force. Gravity pulls everything toward the center of Earth, creating the near ball-like shape. Centrifugal force moves things away from the center of Earth. As Earth revolves, the centrifugal force at the equator is greater than at the poles. This difference in centrifugal force causes Earth to be flatter at the poles than at the equator.

MASS OR WEIGHT

Earth is composed of matter. When all the matter is put together, it is called *mass*. Earth's mass or weight is approximately 6,000,000,000,000,000,000,000 metric tons. This number is read as, "six sextillion metric tons."

Henry Cavendish was the first person to calculate correctly the mass of Earth. He did this sometime during the 1790s, without the benefit of modern equipment. Scientists agree that Henry Cavendish's estimates are very close to today's scientific estimates.

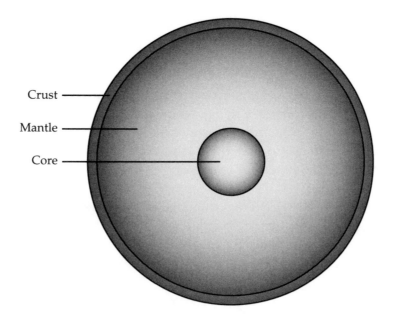

Crust ———

Mantle ———

Core ———

LAYERS

We know about Earth's surface but much less about what is inside Earth. If Earth were cut in half, you would be able to see three different layers. Near the surface you would see the *crust*. It varies in thickness from 3 miles at the deepest parts of the ocean to 22 miles under the continents.

The second layer you would see is the *mantle*. The mantle goes to a depth of 1,800 miles. Like the crust, it is made of solid rock.

At the center of Earth is the *core*. It is about 2,100 miles in radius. Although the inner core is believed to be solid, it is surrounded by a liquid. The core is mostly iron, with some nickel and silicon.

ATMOSPHERE

Earth is surrounded by a large blanket of air called the *atmosphere*. The atmosphere revolves with Earth. This atmosphere is made of several gases. The most common gases are nitrogen (78%) and oxygen (21%). Gases like carbon dioxide, water vapor, and others make up the remaining one percent.

These gases are held near Earth by gravity. The atmosphere is heavier near the surface of Earth. The air is *heavy* near the surface and gets *thinner* as we move away from the surface into space. Half of the atmosphere is found within 3.5 miles of Earth's surface.

CHANGES

Earth's surface is always changing. The way it looks today is not the way it looked when Earth was formed. Changes come about slowly and are difficult to see in a human lifetime. Sometimes, however, changes come about rapidly, as when Mount Saint Helens erupted in 1980 in the Cascade Range, located in the southwestern part of the state of Washington.

It is not only the surface of Earth that changes. The continents move and the size of oceans, seas, lakes, and streams changes with them. The crust of Earth sits on six very large plates. These plates move slowly. When they collide, large mountain chains develop. When they move away from each other, large oceans appear.

SUMMARY

Earth is shaped like a ball but not perfectly. Its shape is determined by both gravity and centrifugal force. It weighs six sextillion metric tons. Its thickness varies from 3 to 22 miles and it is surrounded by an atmosphere made of gases. It is in constant change. What you see today is not what you would have seen when Earth was formed.

QUESTION–ANSWER NOTETAKING FORM

Name: _____Mary_____

Title:	*Earth*
Heading:	Shape
Question:	What is the shape of Earth?
Answer:	Like a ball but not perfectly round
Question:	What determined the shape of Earth?
Answer:	Gravity and centrifugal force
Heading:	Mass or weight
Question:	What is mass?
Answer:	All matter put together
Question:	How much does Earth weigh?
Answer:	Approximately six sextillion metric tons
Question:	Who was the first person to calculate the mass of Earth?
Answer:	Henry Cavendish, during the 1790s
Heading:	Layers
Question:	How many layers does Earth have?
Answer:	Three
Question:	What are they?
Answer:	Crust, mantle, core
Heading:	Atmosphere
Question:	What is the atmosphere of Earth made of?
Answer:	A number of gases: nitrogen 78%, oxygen 21%, other gases 1%
Question:	What keeps the gases near Earth's surface?
Answer:	Gravity
Heading:	Changes
Question:	How does Earth change?
Answer:	Sometimes slowly, sometimes rapidly, such as when a volcano like Mount Saint Helens erupted
Question:	What is one cause of changes in bodies of water?
Answer:	Movement of the continents
Question:	What causes the continents to move?
Answer:	The continents sit on six large plates that move slowly.
Question:	How do mountain chains form?
Answer:	They form when plates collide.
Question:	How do large oceans form?
Answer:	They form when plates move away from one another.

Survey the following textbook chapter. Form one or more **Questions** for each heading. Write each question on the Question–Answer Notetaking Form. **Read** to find the answer to each question. **Write** the answer to each question on the Question–Answer Notetaking Form. The first two questions and answers are provided for you.

Money

Money is some type of paper bill or metal coin that people use to exchange for things they want to purchase or accept for a job that they do. Most modern money consists of paper bills and coins made of copper, nickel, or other metals. Bills and coins from different countries have various appearances and a variety of names.

USES OF MONEY

Money is used in several ways. The most important function of money is as a medium of exchange. This means that people will accept money in exchange for their goods and services. If money were not available as a medium of exchange, people would have to use the barter system. For example, if you wanted a new jacket, you would have to barter for it by finding something the store owner would accept in exchange, perhaps some vegetables or fruit grown in your garden. Barterning can be inconvenient and time-consuming.

Money also serves as a unit of account. People relate the value of goods and services to a sum of money. In the United States, *dollars* are used to indicate price

---

in the same way that *gallons* are used to measure volume of liquid and *miles* are used to measure distance.

A third function of money is as a way of storing wealth. People are accustomed to saving money to use for future purchases. Stocks, bonds, real estate, gold, and jewels are also considered to be stores of wealth.

MAKING MONEY CONVENIENT TO USE

Money should be convenient to use. It should be available in pieces of standard value so that the pieces do not have to be weighed or measured individually each time they are needed. It should be carried easily so that people can transport it to purchase what they need. Money should be easily divided into units so that people can make small purchases and receive change if needed. The beads, cocoa beans, salt, shells, and tobacco used in the past for money do not meet the criteria of convenience when applied to modern uses of money.

THE BARTER SYSTEM

The barter system of trading was used by most primitive people because they learned by experience that almost everyone was willing to accept certain goods in exchange for products or services. The goods they exchanged included salt, animal hides, cattle, cloth, and articles of gold and silver. These early people used the merchandise they bartered as a medium of exchange in a manner similar to our use of money today.

COINS COME INTO USE

The Lydians, a people who lived in what is now western Turkey, are credited with the invention of the first metal coins, sometime around 600 B.C. The bean-shaped coins were a natural mixture of gold and silver, called *electrum*. The electrum were stamped with a design to show that the King of Lydia guaranteed them to be of uniform size. These coins became a medium of exchange accepted by traders instead of cattle, cloth, or gold dust. When other countries recognized the convenience of the Lydian coins, they devised metal money of their own. Today's coins are modeled after the early Lydian prototypes. Modern coins, not unlike the coins of ancient Lydia, have a government-approved design and a value stamped on their face.

PAPER MONEY BEGINS TO BE USED

Paper money originated in China during the seventh century. Even though the Italian trader, Marco Polo, exposed Europeans to this Chinese innovation, Europeans could not understand how a piece of paper could be valuable. They did not use paper money until the 1600s, when banks began to issue paper bills called *bank notes* to depositors and borrowers.

The American colonists did not use paper currency. They had to buy products from the English traders with *bills of exchange*. These were documents received from English traders in exchange for goods. It was not until the Revolutionary War that the American Continental Congress issued paper money to help finance the war for independence. From that time forward, the United States used paper money.

CONCLUSION

Today, it would be very difficult to buy and sell the products available in stores without money. Paper and coin money make it easy and quick to purchase a variety of consumer goods. Imagine what your day would be like if you had to barter for lunch, gasoline, or a ticket to see a movie or sports event.

QUESTION–ANSWER NOTETAKING FORM: "MONEY"

Question: How is money used?

Answer: As a medium of exchange, a unit of account, and a store of wealth.

Question: What is done to make money easy to use?

Answer: Made available in pieces of standard value, easy to carry, and easy to divide into units.

Question: _____

Answer: _____

Question: _____

Answer: _____

Question: _____

Answer: _____

Question: _____

Answer: _____

Question: _____

Answer: _____

Question: _____

Answer: _____

Question: _____

Answer: _____

Apply what you learned about SQRW to this chapter and complete the Question–Answer Note-taking Form.

Amphibians

From a scientific standpoint, amphibians are an interesting class of vertebrate animals. The class Amphibia appeared in the process of evolution between the fishes and the reptiles. Amphibians were the first vertebrates to make their way from an aquatic environment to life on land. They combine characteristics of both land and water animals. The amphibians of today live part of their life on land but must return to the water in order to reproduce.

HOW AMPHIBIANS EVOLVED

Scientists believe that for millions of years animals lived only in a water environment. There were periodic droughts in which much of the water dried up. Although many varieties of fish existed at this time, only those fish that could withstand drought conditions were able to survive.

The fish that were able to adapt to a drier environment had muscular fins that allowed them to dig deeper into the drying water source. Some were able to move across land from one water hole to another. They often had lungs that allowed them to breathe out of water. The fish that had these land-adaptive characteristics survived the droughts and multiplied to produce new generations of animals. These animals are the ancestors of modern amphibians.

CHARACTERISTICS OF AMPHIBIANS

The name *amphibian* comes from the Greek *amphi,* meaning "both," and *bios* meaning "life." This is descriptive of the two stages of existence of amphibians. The young are similar to fish. They can live only in water. As they mature, they change into land-dwelling creatures. Their adult forms combine gills, lungs, fins, and legs.

Amphibians differ from other vertebrates in several ways. They have smooth skin, which is thin and usually moist, instead of scales, fur, or feathers. If they have feet, they are webbed. Their toes are soft and do not have claws. The larval forms of the young are usually vegetarian, but the adults are carnivorous. Amphibians breathe with gills, lungs, and skin. They change from a fishlike creature to an animal that can live in water and on land. This is a unique trait of amphibians.

CLASSIFICATIONS

The class Amphibia is made up of three distinct *orders*. Order Apoda consists of wormlike animals with short or no tails and no legs. They live in tropical areas. Order Caudata includes amphibians such as newts and salamanders. These animals have elongated bodies and proportioned tails, usually with two pairs of limbs. The most familiar amphibians belong to the order Anura. Frogs and toads and other members of this class have short tailless bodies in their adult stage. They have two pairs of limbs, with the hind legs adapted for leaping. Anura have gills in the larval stage and lungs in the adult stage.

SALAMANDERS

One group of amphibians, the Caudata, are represented primarily by salamanders. Salamanders resemble lizards because they both have long bodies, short legs, and long tails. Salamanders, unlike lizards, have soft moist skin and lack the claws of their reptilian look-alikes.

Salamanders are found in wet or moist areas because they cannot survive where it is dry. These amphibians do not seem to have much protection from predators. They try to protect themselves by giving off a bad-tasting substance and by changing their colors so they are difficult to see.

FROGS AND TOADS

The most familiar amphibians are the countless frogs and toads found near the ponds and streams in all rural areas of the country. Frogs and toads are similar and are often mistaken for each other. However, they differ in several ways.

The toad enjoys life on land. It begins as an egg fertilized in the water, but soon after hatching, it changes from a tadpole to an adult toad. Then it spends most of its time on land. This brown, warty creature returns to the water only to lay its eggs.

Frogs differ from toads in their preference for a watery habitat. Frogs usually live very near water, frequently around ponds and marshes. Bullfrogs and leopard frogs are the most common frogs in the United States.

CONCLUSION

You can see why amphibians are an interesting class of vertebrates. No other animals are as comfortable both in water and on land. Their unique evolution provides a rich field of study for marine scientists.

QUESTION–ANSWER NOTETAKING FORM: "AMPHIBIANS"

Question: _____

Answer: _____

Question: _____

Answer: _____

Question: _____

Answer: _____

Question: _____

Answer: _____

Question: _____

Answer: _____

Question: _____

Answer: _____

Question: _____

Answer: _____

Question: _____

Answer: _____

Question: _____

Answer: _____

Fill in the words to complete this paragraph that describes how to use SQRW.

To survey a textbook chapter, you begin by reading the (1) _____ to

identify the general topic of the chapter. Next, read the (2) _____

to get an overview of the chapter. You will find this in the first one or two

(3) _____ of the chapter. Then read the (4) _____

to learn about the specific topics that will be covered. Finally, read the summary or the

(5) _____ found at the end of the chapter. In the question step, use

the words (6) _____ , (7) _____ ,

(8) _____ , (9) _____ , (10) _____ ,

or (11) _____ to change (12) _____ into questions.

The next step is to (13) _____ to find answers to the questions.

Last, (14) _____ the answers on the Question–Answer Note-

taking Form.

Reflection How has the SQRW strategy made you a better student?

_____

_____

_____

_____

_____

_____

_____

ANSWER KEY FOR CHAPTER TWO

2-1 Words underlined by students will vary.

2-2 No writing required.

2-3 Possible questions and answers for each heading are:

Heading:	Uses of Money
Question:	How is money used?
Answer:	Money is used as a medium of exchange, a unit of account, and a store of wealth.

Heading:	Making Money Convenient to Use
Question:	What is done to make money easy to use?
Answer:	It must be available in pieces of standard value, it should be easy to carry, and it should be easy to divide into units.
Question:	What are some examples of things not easy to use as money?
Answer:	Beads, beans, salt, shells, and tobacco

Heading:	The Barter System
Question:	What is the barter system?
Answer:	A way to exchange goods for products or services
Question:	Who used the barter system?
Answer:	Primitive people
Question:	What are examples of goods used in the barter system?
Answer:	Salt, animal hides, cattle, cloth, and articles made of gold or silver

Heading:	Coins Come into Use
Question:	When did coins come into use?
Answer:	Sometime around 600 B.C.
Question:	Who invented coins?
Answer:	The Lydians, who lived in what is now western Turkey
Question:	What is "electrum"?
Answer:	A mixture of gold and silver used to make coins
Question:	What is stamped on the face of modern coins?
Answer:	Government-approved design and a value

Heading:	Paper Money Begins to Be Used
Question:	When did paper money begin to be used?
Answer:	The 1600s
Question:	Where did paper money originate?
Answer:	China
Question:	Why didn't the early Europeans use paper money?
Answer:	They could not understand how paper could be valuable.
Question:	When was paper money first used in America?
Answer:	At the beginning of the Revolutionary War

2-4 Possible questions and answers for each heading are:

Heading:	How Amphibians Evolved
Question:	How did amphibians evolve?
Answer:	They evolved by adapting to a dryer environment caused by droughts.
Question:	What are the characteristics of fish that evolved into amphibians?
Answer:	Muscular fins and lungs

Heading:	Characteristics of Amphibians
Question:	What are the characteristics of amphibians?
Answer:	1. Smooth skin that is thin and moist
	2. Webbed feet
	3. Soft toes without claws
	4. Vegetarian at birth, but carnivorous as adults
	5. Breathe with gills, lungs, and skin
	6. Live in water and on land

Question:	What is the most distinctive characteristic of amphibians?
Answer:	Their ability to live both in the water and on land
Question:	Where does the word *amphibian* come from?
Answer:	From the Greek words *amphi* and *bios*

Heading:	Classifications
Question:	What are the classifications of amphibians?
Answer:	Apoda, Caudata, Anura

Heading:	Salamanders
Question:	What are salamanders?
Answer:	They are amphibians of the Caudata class.
Question:	What do salamanders resemble?
Answer:	Lizards
Question:	Where can salamanders be found?
Answer:	In wet or moist areas
Question:	How do salamanders protect themselves?
Answers:	They give off a bad-tasting substance and change colors.

Heading:	Frogs and Toads
Question:	What is the difference between frogs and toads?
Answer:	Frogs spend most of their time in or near water. Toads prefer to be on land.
Question:	What are the names of the two most common types of frogs found in the United States?
Answer:	Bullfrogs, leopard frogs

2-5 1. title. 2. introduction. 3. paragraphs. 4. headings. 5. conclusion. 6. who. 7. what. 8. where. 9. when. 10. why. 11. how. 12. headings. 13. read. 14. write.

Reflection Responses will vary but should reveal insights into how the student has become a better learner.

## CHAPTER THREE

Interpreting Graphic Aids

TITLES OF REPRODUCIBLE ACTIVITIES

USING THE REPRODUCIBLE ACTIVITIES

After you have distributed a reproducible activity, here are suggestions for its use. Define any terms and clarify any concepts students do not know. Feel free to add further information, illustrations, or examples. Wherever possible, relate the activity to actual subject-area assignments.

3-1 Pictographs

Tell students that graphs are used to show information. Explain that graphs show the relationship between two or more things. Tell students you will be teaching them about four types of graphs. Use this activity to introduce students to pictographs. Then have students use the pictograph to answer the questions.

3-2 Pie Graphs

Tell students the term *pie graph* is used because this type of graph looks like a pie divided into slices. Explain that the parts must add up to 100 percent. Also explain why some pie graphs have a part labeled "Other." Then have students use the pie graph to answer the questions.

3-3 Bar Graphs

Tell students that bar graphs are used to show the relationships between sets of facts. Show students the different parts of a bar graph. Have students use the bar graph to answer the questions.

3-4 Another Type of Bar Graph

Tell students that some bar graphs use horizontal bars to show the relationships between sets of facts. Point out that the length of the bar shows how much the bar stands for. Have students use the bar graph to answer the questions.

3-5 Line Graphs

Explain that line graphs are used to show trends over a period of time. Show students the different parts of a line graph. Have students use the line graph to answer the questions.

3-6 Diagrams

Explain that diagrams show the parts of an object or thing. Point out that diagrams often show how the parts go together or how an object or thing works. Then have students use the diagram to answer the questions.

3-7 Tables

Tell students that tables are used to present facts. Explain the importance of the columns and column headings. Have students use the table to answer the questions.

3-8 Organizational Charts

Tell students that organizational charts show how things are organized. Explain how boxes and lines are used to present information and show relationships. Then have students use the organizational chart to answer the questions.

3-9 Flow Charts

Tell students that flow charts are used to show a process by which something works or occurs. Point out that arrows show the direction or order in which the process happens. Then have students use the flow chart to answer the questions.

3-10 Time Lines

Tell students that a time line shows the relationship between events over time and shows when important things happen. Point out that most time lines are shown from left to right. Have students use the time line to answer the questions.

3-11 Map Legend

Tell students that maps have a legend that explains the meaning of the symbols appearing on the map. Explain that map legends may vary from map to map. Tell students that sometimes a map legend is called a map key. Then have students use the map legend at the bottom of the map to answer the questions about the map shown.

3-12 Map Compass

Tell students that a map compass is used to show directions on a map. Then have students use the map compass to answer the questions about the map shown. Note that the capital is identified by a special symbol.

3-13 Map Scale

Explain that a map scale is used to find the distance between two places on a map. Map scales are often shown in both miles and kilometers. Use the steps provided in the activity to demonstrate how to find the distance between two cities. Then have students use the map scale to answer questions about the map shown.

3-14 Political and Physical Maps

Bring out the unique features of these two types of maps. Have students use what they learned to answer the questions.

3-15 Road Maps

Tell students that a road map shows both major highways and secondary roads. Show students the symbols used to mark the number of the major highways and secondary roads. Also show how major highways appear in darker or bolder ink than secondary roads. Explain how road maps are used when traveling. Then have students use the road map to answer the questions.

3-16 Combining Types of Maps

Review political, physical, and road maps and the use of a legend, compass, and scale. Have students use the map of California to answer the questions.

3-17 Weather Maps

Show how weather maps are used to show present weather conditions and predict future weather conditions. Have students use the weather map to answer the questions.

3-18 Mastery Assessment and Reflection

Have students complete this assessment when you believe they have learned to use and interpret graphic aids. Review the results of the assessment with the students. Provide additional instruction as necessary.

> ### Interpreting Pictographs
>
> **Pictographs** use pictures or symbols to present information. Each picture or symbol stands for an amount of something. A pictograph has a title that tells you what it shows. It also has a key that explains what each picture stands for.

Examine this pictograph and answer the questions.

Speed of Animals

Cheetah	🐈🐈🐈🐈🐈🐈🐈
Grizzly bear	🐈🐈🐈
Deer	🐈🐈🐈
Black mamba snake	🐈🐈
Lion	🐈🐈🐈🐈🐈
Cat	🐈🐈🐈
Pig	🐈
Zebra	🐈🐈🐈🐈
Fox	🐈🐈🐈🐈
Dragonfly	🐈🐈🐈🐈🐈🐈

Key: 🐈 = 10 miles per hour

---

1. What does this pictograph show? _____

2. What does 🐈 stand for? _____

3. Which is the slowest animal? _____

4. Which is the fastest animal? _____

5. Which animals can travel at least 40 miles per hour? _____

6. Which animals travel faster than a deer? _____

7. Which animals travel slower than a grizzly bear? _____

8. What does 🐈🐈 stand for? _____

9. How many more miles per hour does a zebra travel than a deer? _____

10. Which animal travels exactly twice as fast as a deer? _____

Interpreting Pie Graphs

Pie graphs look like a pie divided into slices. The title tells the subject of the pie graph. Each part of a pie graph shows how much of the whole it stands for. The parts must equal the whole and must add up to 100 percent. Very small parts are often combined and called "Other." This is done because it is difficult to show a very small part of something.

Examine this pie graph and answer the questions.

Chemical Elements in the Human Body

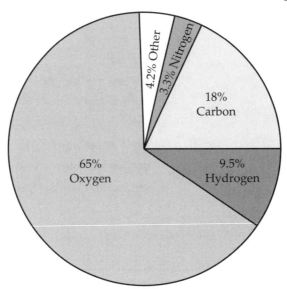

1. What does this pie graph show? _____

2. Which chemical is found in the greatest amount in the human body? _____

3. Is there a higher amount of hydrogen or carbon in the human body? _____

4. Oxygen plus carbon make up what percentage of the chemical elements in the human body? _____

5. About one-fifth of the chemical elements in the body consist of which element? _____

6. Oxygen and hydrogen combine to form water in the human body. What percentage of the human body is water? _____

7. The parts shown in a pie graph must add up to what percent? _____

8. Why is there a category called "Other"? _____

Interpreting Bar Graphs

Bar graphs show the relationships between sets of facts. A bar graph has a title at the top. The label on the left tells what the numbers stand for. The label on the bottom tells what the bars stand for. Going up the left side is a number line. The height of each bar shows how much it stands for. Look at the height of two or more bars to make comparisons.

Look at the bar graph and answer the questions that follow.

Most Popular Tourist Attractions, by Number of Visitors, 1997

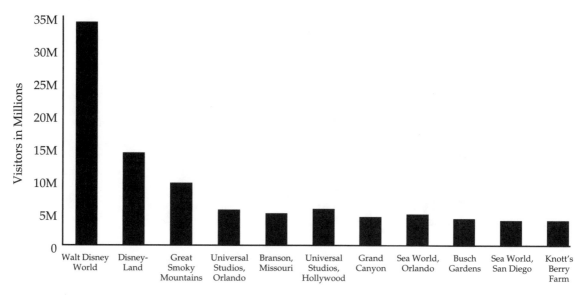

1. What is this bar graph about? _____

2. What do the bars stand for? _____

3. What do the numbers stand for? _____

4. Which tourist attraction had the most visitors in 1997? _____

5. Which tourist attraction had ten million visitors? _____

6. Which tourist attraction had more visitors, Busch Gardens or Disneyland? _____

Interpreting Bar Graphs

The bar graph on this page shows information using horizontal bars. The label on the left tells what each bar stands for. The label on the bottom tells what the numbers stand for. The length of each bar shows how much it stands for. Look at the length of two or more bars to make comparisons.

Look at the bar graph and answer the questions that follow.

Endangered Species, 1998: U.S. vs. the World

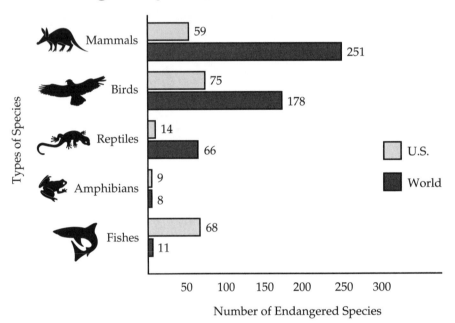

Source: U.S. Fish and Wildlife Service

1. What is this bar graph about? _____

2. What do the pictures stand for? _____

3. What do the numbers stand for? _____

4. How many endangered species are there in the United States? Are there more endangered species in the United States than in the rest of the world? _____

5. What is the most endangered species in the United States? _____

   The world? _____

6. Which species are more endangered in the world than in the United States? _____

7. Which is the least endangered species in the United States? _____

Interpreting Line Graphs

Line graphs show the relationships between sets of facts. A line graph has a title at the top. The label on the left tells what the numbers stand for. The label on the bottom tells what the dots stand for. Going up the left side is a number line. The height of each dot shows how much it stands for. The dots are connected by a line. The line shows how a trend is developing or how things are changing.

Look at the line graph and answer the questions that follow.

American Foreign Trade, 1865–1915

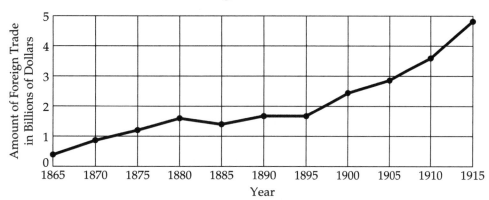

Source: U.S. government

1. What is the line graph about? _____

2. What do the dots stand for? _____

3. What do the numbers on the left side stand for? _____

4. What was the amount of foreign trade in 1880? _____

5. In 1905? _____

6. In 1915? _____

7. What happened to the amount of foreign trade from 1875 to 1880? _____

8. From 1880 to 1885? _____

9. During which five-year period was foreign trade greatest? _____

10. What was the trend in foreign trade from 1865 to 1915? _____

Interpreting Diagrams

Diagrams are drawings of an object. A diagram shows the parts of the object. The parts are labeled. Often a diagram shows how the parts go together or how the object works.

Look at the following diagram and answer the questions.

A Dry Cell Battery

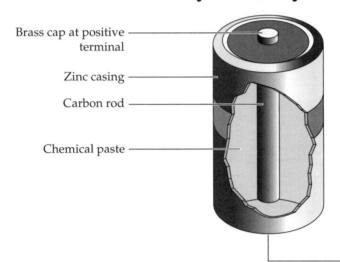

Brass cap at positive terminal

Zinc casing

Carbon rod

Chemical paste

Negative terminal

1. What is the title of this diagram? _____

2. How many parts of the battery are shown? _____

3. Which part is in the center of the battery? _____

4. Which part is at the top of the battery? _____

5. Which part is at the bottom of the battery? _____

6. Which part is on the outside of the battery? _____

7. What material surrounds the carbon rod? _____

Interpreting Tables

Tables are used to present facts. A table has a title that explains its purpose. In the table are columns, each of which has a heading that tells what facts you will find in that column.

Look at the following table and answer the questions.

The Sun and Its Planets

Names of Planets	Miles from Sun	Orbit Time
Mercury	36 million	88 days
Venus	67 million	224 days
Earth	93 million	365.25 days
Mars	142 million	687 days
Jupiter	483 million	11.9 years
Saturn	887 million	29.5 years
Uranus	1,783 million	84 years
Neptune	2,794 million	164.8 years
Pluto	3,666 million	247.7 years

1. What is the title of this table? _____

2. What information is presented in the first column? _____

3. In the second column? _____

4. In the third column? _____

5. How many miles is Earth from the Sun? _____

6. How many miles is Neptune from the Sun? _____

7. How long does it take Earth to orbit around the Sun? _____

8. Which planet has the shortest orbit? _____

9. Which has the longest? _____

10. Which planet is farthest from the Sun? _____

11. Which two planets are closer to the Sun than Earth? _____

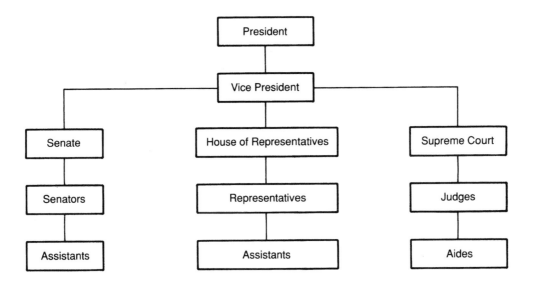

Interpreting Organizational Charts

Organizational charts are used to show how things are organized. Information is presented in boxes. Each box is labeled to show what it presents. Lines are used to show how the boxes are related.

Look at the following organizational chart. It shows how the U.S. government is organized to do its work. The boxes contain facts about the government. The lines show how the facts go together. By studying the chart, you can see how the government works.

U.S. Government

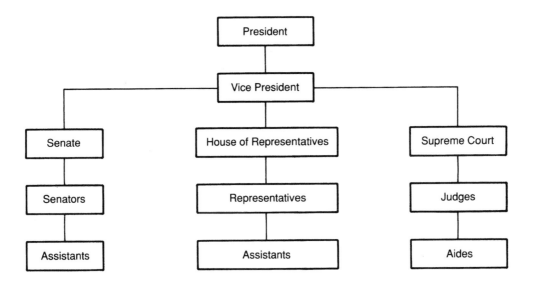

Use the chart to answer these questions:

1. Who is the highest-ranking official in the United States government? _____

2. Who works in the Senate? _____

3. Who works in the House of Representatives? _____

4. Who works in the Supreme Court? _____

5. Which official is directly below the president? _____

6. Where do aides work? _____

7. For whom do assistants work? _____

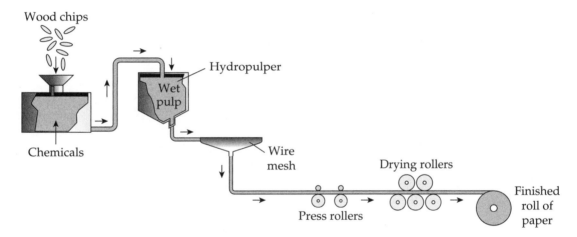

Interpreting Flow Charts

Flow charts are used to show a process by which something works or happens. Information is presented with drawings and arrows. Statements are used to show what is happening at each stage in the process. The arrows show the direction or order in which the process happens.

Look at the flow chart. It shows how paper is made from wood. Read the title and the statements. Study the drawings. Use the arrows to learn the order of the steps in the process of turning wood into paper. Then answer the questions.

How Wood Becomes Paper

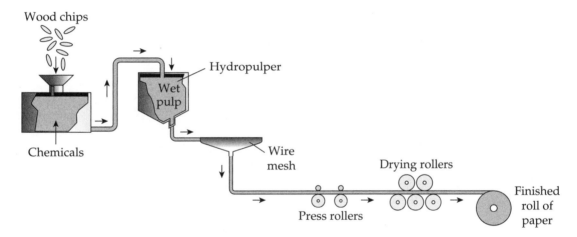

1. What is the title of this flow chart? _____

2. What process is being shown in this flow chart? _____

3. What is the first step in the process? _____

4. Second step? _____

5. Third step? _____

6. Fourth step? _____

7. Fifth step? _____

8. What product is produced at the end of this process? _____

Interpreting Time Lines

A **time line** shows the relationship between events over time. It also shows when important events happened. Most time lines run from left to right. The left side of the time line is the earliest time and the right side is the most recent time.

Major Events of the U.S. Civil War

1861	1862	1863	1864	1865
Civil War begins as Confederates fire on Fort Sumter	Ironclad ships *Monitor* and *Merrimac* battle	Battle of Gettysburg	Grant named Commander Union Army	Confederates surrender

Look at the time line and answer the questions that follow.

1. What is the title? _____

2. What time period is shown? _____

3. What was the first major event? _____

   _____

4. The last? _____

5. In what year did the battle of Gettysburg occur? _____

6. What event occurred the year before the battle of Gettysburg? _____

   _____

7. In what year did the Civil War begin? _____

   End? _____

Interpreting a Map Legend

A **map legend** tells you the meaning of each symbol used on a map. Because different maps contain different information, the symbols may be different from map to map. This means that the legend is different from map to map. On some maps, the map legend is called a **map key**. A map legend or key is usually at the bottom of a map.

Use this map and its legend to answer the questions that follow.

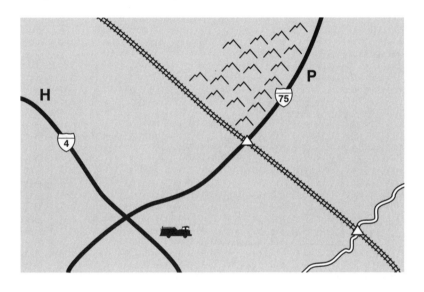

Road   Railroad   Mountains   River   **H** Hospital

Fire station   **P** Police station   △ Bridge   Highway number

1. Where is a map legend usually found? _____

2. How many highways are shown on this map? _____

3. Next to which highway is the fire station? _____

4. Along which highway is the hospital? _____

5. How many bridges are there? _____

6. Which highway do the railroad tracks cross? _____

7. Along what highway is the police station? _____

8. How do trains get across the river? _____

9. Which is closer to the river—the fire station or the hospital? _____

10. What is closest to where two highways meet? _____

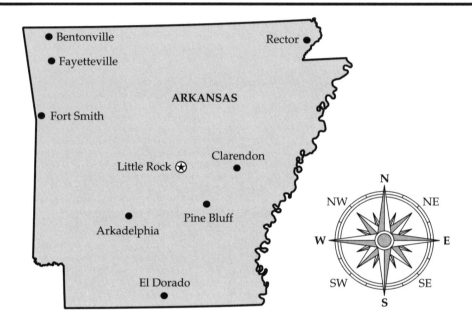 **3-12**

Interpreting a Map Compass

A **map compass** shows you directions on a map. It shows you north (N), south (S), east (E), west (W), and the directions in between: northeast (NE), southeast (SE), and so on. Use the map of Arkansas and the map compass to answer the questions that follow.

In what direction would you travel to go from Little Rock to each of the following cities?

1. Fayetteville _____

2. El Dorado _____

3. Clarendon _____

4. Rector _____

In what direction would you travel if you went from

5. Pine Bluff to Arkadelphia? _____

6. Bentonville to Fort Smith? _____

7. El Dorado to Little Rock? _____

8. Fort Smith to Rector? _____

Which city is farthest

9. east? _____

10. west? _____

11. north? _____

12. south? _____

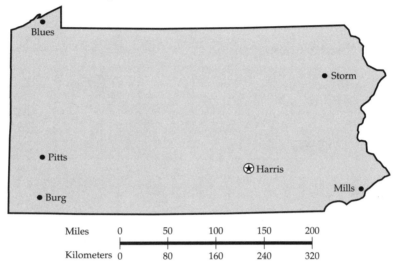

Interpreting a Map Scale

The **map scale** shows distance on a map. It may tell distance in miles, in kilometers, or in both miles and kilometers. Use a map scale to find how far it is from one place to another.

Here is a map with cities and a map scale:

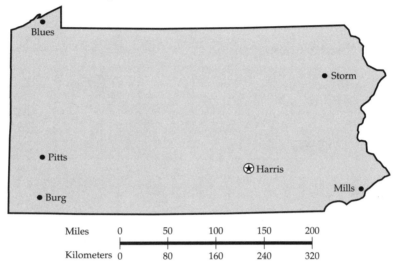

Here are the steps to follow to find the distance between two cities:
- Place the edge of a piece of paper between any two cities shown on the map.
- Make a mark on the paper by each city.
- Lay the paper on the scale to find how far it is between the two marks. This will tell you how far it is between the two cities.

Follow these steps to answer these questions.

1. How many kilometers is equal to 100 miles? _____

2. How many miles is it from Mills to Pitts? _____ How many kilometers? _____

3. How many miles is it from Blues to Pitts? _____ How many kilometers? _____

4. How far is it between Blues and Harris in miles? _____

5. How far is it between Harris and Storm in kilometers? _____

6. Which two cities are closest? _____ How many miles is it from one to the other? _____

7. Which two cities are farthest apart? _____ How many kilometers is it from one to the other? _____

8. Which two cities are farther apart—Burg and Pitts or Storm and Pitts? _____

Interpreting Political and Physical Maps

A **political map** has lines that show political or government boundaries. Look at the political map of South America, which shows the countries on that continent.

A **physical map** shows the features of Earth's surface, such as mountains, highlands, plateaus, deserts, and major bodies of water. Look at the physical map of South America and find these features. No political boundaries are shown.

Political Map of South America

Physical Map of South America

Which type of map would you use to

1. identify the provinces in Canada? _____

2. identify major mountain ranges? _____

3. write a report on the major oceans of the world? _____

4. answer a question about the new countries in eastern Europe? _____

5. locate the Nile River? _____

6. learn which countries border France? _____

Interpreting Road Maps

A **road map** shows the major highways and the secondary roads for a geographical area. The major highways are identified with dark lines and the secondary roads with light lines. Both types of roads have symbols showing the number or name of the highway or road. Road maps are used to show how to get from one place to another. Here is a sample road map.

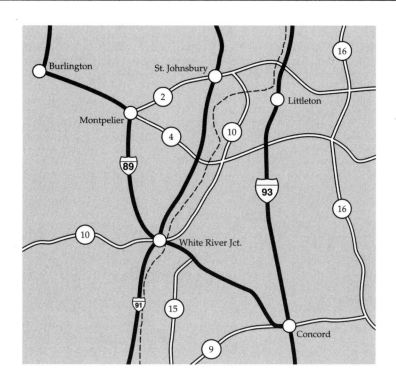

1. What do dark lines identify? _____

2. Light lines? _____

3. What major highway would you take to travel between Burlington and Concord? _____

4. What direct route takes you from Concord to Littleton? _____

5. What community do you find where 91 and 2 meet? _____

6. What community do you find where routes 10, 89, and 91 cross? _____

7. What two major highways will take you to Concord? _____

8. How many highways are shown? What are their numbers? _____

9. How many secondary roads are shown? What are their numbers? _____

10. Does a highway pass through Littleton? _____

Here is a map of California that combines features of political, physical, and road maps. It has a legend, compass, and scale. Use the map to answer the questions.

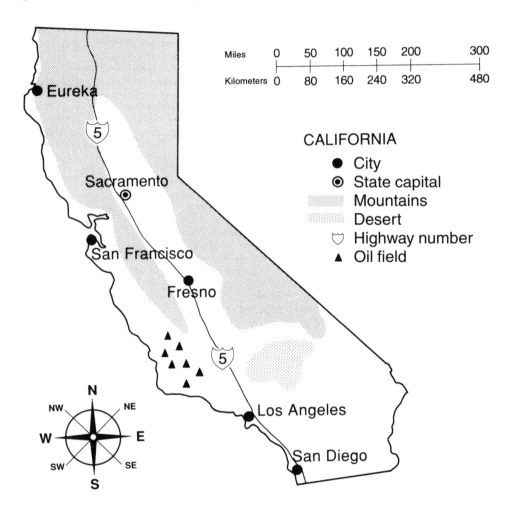

1. Between which two cities are oil fields located? _____

2. What is the distance in kilometers between San Francisco and Los Angeles? _____

3. What is the state capital? _____

4. In which direction would you travel from San Francisco to Fresno? _____

5. What highway runs north and south? _____

Maps can be used to tell information about the weather. Use the legend and compass to answer the questions.

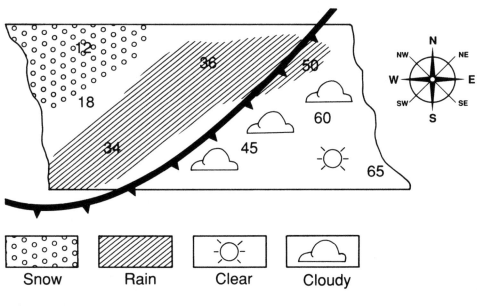

What is the predicted weather for these areas?

1. SE _____

2. NE _____

3. NW _____

4. SW _____

5. In which area is the coldest temperature? _____

6. In which area is the warmest temperature? _____

7. What will the weather be like in the SE area in a day or two? _____

Mastery Assessment and Reflection

Directions   Show what you have learned about using and interpreting graphic aids by writing an answer for each of the following:

1. What is used to show an amount of something in a pictograph? _____

2. In a pie graph, what percent must the parts equal? _____

3. What do bar graphs show? _____

4. What type of graph is used to show trends over a period of time? _____

5. What type of drawing shows the parts of some object or thing? _____

6. What type of graphic aid shows facts arranged in columns? _____

7. What type of chart shows how things are organized? _____

8. What type of chart shows how something works? _____

9. What type of graphic aid is used to show when important events happened? _____

10. Tell what each type of map shows:

   a. Political _____

   b. Physical _____

   c. Road _____

   d. Weather _____

11. What is each of the following used for on a map?

   a. Legend _____

   b. Compass _____

   c. Scale _____

Reflection   How has being able to interpret graphic aids made you a better student?

_____

_____

ANSWER KEY FOR CHAPTER THREE

3-1 1. Speed of animals.   2. 10 mph.   3. Pig.   4. Cheetah.   5. Zebra, cheetah, lion, dragonfly, and fox.   6. Cheetah, lion, zebra, fox, and dragonfly.   7. Black mamba snake and pig.   8. 20 mph.   9. 10 mph.   10. Dragonfly.

3-2 1. Chemical elements in the human body.   2. Oxygen.   3. Carbon.   4. 83%.   5. Carbon.   6. 74.5%.   7. 100%.   8. Because it is difficult to show very small parts.

3-3 1. The most popular tourist attractions in 1997.   2. Tourist attractions.   3. Visitors in millions.   4. Walt Disney World.   5. Great Smoky Mountains.   6. Disneyland.

3-4 1. Endangered species in the United States and the world.   2. Types of species.   3. Number of each endangered species.   4. 225; No.   5. Birds; mammals.   6. Mammals, birds, reptiles.   7. Amphibians.

3-5 1. American foreign trade from 1865 to 1915.   2. How much foreign trade there was.   3. Amount of foreign trade in billions of dollars.   4. About 1.5 billion dollars.   5. About 2.9 billion dollars.   6. About 4.9 billion dollars.   7. Increased.   8. Decreased slightly.   9. 1910–1915.   10. Increased.

3-6 1. A Dry Cell Battery.   2. 5.   3. Carbon rod.   4. Brass cap.   5. Negative terminal.   6. Zinc casing.   7. Chemical paste.

3-7 1. The Sun and Its Planets.   2. Names of planets.   3. Miles from Sun.   4. Orbit time.   5. 93 million.   6. 2,794 million.   7. 365.25 days.   8. Mercury.   9. Pluto.   10. Pluto.   11. Mercury and Venus.

3-8 1. President.   2. Senators and assistants.   3. Representatives and assistants.   4. Judges and aides.   5. Vice president.   6. In the Supreme Court.   7. Senators and representatives.

3-9 1. How Wood Becomes Paper.   2. The process by which wood is turned into paper.   3. Putting wood chips into the chemical container.   4. Making wet pulp in the hydropulper.   5. Running the wet pulp through the wire mesh.   6. Running the wet pulp through the press rollers.   7. Running the wet pulp through dry rollers.   8. Roll of paper.

3-10 1. Major Events of the U.S. Civil War.   2. 1861–1865.   3. Confederates fire on Fort Sumter and war begins.   4. Confederates surrender.   5. 1863.   6. Battle between *Monitor* and *Merrimac*.   7. 1861; 1865.

3-11 1. Bottom of a map.   2. Two.   3. Highway 4.   4. Highway 4.   5. Two.   6. Highway 75.   7. Highway 75.   8. Cross a bridge.   9. Fire station.   10. Fire station.

3-12 1. NW.   2. S.   3. E.   4. NE.   5. W.   6. S.   7. N.   8. NE.   9. Rector.   10. Fort Smith.   11. Bentonville.   12. El Dorado.

3-13 1. 160 kilometers.   2. Approximately 340 miles; 530 kilometers.   3. Approximately 145 miles; 230 kilometers.   4. Approximately 260 miles.   5. Approximately 220 kilometers.   6. Pitts and Burg; approximately 45 miles.   7. Blues and Mills; approximately 590 kilometers.   8. Storm and Pitts.

3-14 1. Political map.   2. Physical map.   3. Physical map.   4. Political map.   5. Physical map.   6. Political map.

3-15 1. Major highways.   2. Secondary roads.   3. Highway 89.   4. Highway 93.   5. St. Johnsbury.   6. White River Junction.   7. Highways 93 and 89.   8. Three highways: 89, 91, 93.   9. Six secondary roads: 2, 16, 4, 10, 15, 9.   10. Yes.

3-16 1. San Francisco and Los Angeles.   2. Approximately 580 kilometers.   3. Sacramento.   4. SE.   5. Highway 5.

3-17 1. Clear.   2. Cloudy and rain.   3. Snow.   4. Rain.   5. NW.   6. SE.
7. Cloudy, possible rain turning to snow, colder.

3-18 1. Pictures or symbols.   2. The whole (100%).   3. Relationships between sets of facts.
4. Line graph.   5. Diagram.   6. Table.   7. Organizational chart.   8. Flow chart.
9. Time line.   10. a. Political or government boundaries.   b. Features of the earth's
surface.   c. Major highways and secondary roads.   d. Current and predicted weather.
11. a. To explain the symbols on a map.   b. To tell directions on a map.   c. To tell
distance on a map.

Reflection   Responses will vary but should reveal insights into how the student has become
a better learner.

CHAPTER FOUR

Taking Notes in Class

TITLES OF REPRODUCIBLE ACTIVITIES

USING THE REPRODUCIBLE ACTIVITIES

After you have distributed a reproducible activity, here are suggestions for its use. Define any terms and clarify any concepts students do not know. Feel free to add further information, illustrations, or examples. Whenever possible, relate the activity to actual subject-area assignments.

4-1 Thinking about How I Take Notes

Tell students that to take good notes in class they must do some things before they arrive at class, some things during class, and some things after

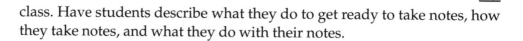

class. Have students describe what they do to get ready to take notes, how they take notes, and what they do with their notes.

4-2 Stages of Notetaking

Have students reread what they wrote in 4-1. Then have them read about the three stages of notetaking, as you explain what to do in each stage. Answer questions students may have. Have students circle Yes for each idea included in 4-1.

4-3 Signal Words

Introduce the signal words *first, second, next,* and *finally.* Tell students these words signal that what follows is important to write in their notes. Have students locate these signal words in "Losing Your Hair." Have students use a variety of signal words when writing their paragraphs.

4-4 Signal Statements

Introduce statements teachers use to signal important information. Have students add others. Then have students identify signal statements in "The Roman Army" and list signal statements they use.

4-5 Abbreviating Words

Tell students that a good way to increase notetaking speed is by abbreviating words as they write. Use the examples to demonstrate how words can be abbreviated. Then have students complete the activity on their own.

4-6 Abbreviating Statements

Tell students they can sometimes abbreviate entire statements. Use the examples to demonstrate how this is done. Then have students complete the activity.

4-7 Using Symbols

Tell students that another way to increase their writing speed is by using symbols. Review the examples provided. Add other examples from materials you are using in your teaching. Have students complete the activity by rewriting the sentences in a shorter form, using abbreviations and symbols.

4-8 Using the Fewest Words

Tell students that teachers usually talk faster than students write. To capture the important points in a lecture, students should write in short sentences or phrases. Have students rewrite the sentences into shorter sentences or phrases.

4-9 Two Common Lecture Styles

Tell students that teachers use different styles when they lecture. Tell them that teachers often use the Topic–Subtopic–Detail (TSD) style or Question–Answer–Detail (QAD) style. Use the page to familiarize students with each style. Conclude by having students write a statement that tells the difference between TSD and QAD.

4-10 TSD Lecture Style

Familiarize students with the procedure by marking the lecture "Sources of Conflict," and have students read and mark the lecture. Then have students complete the notetaking format.

4-11 QAD Lecture Style

Familiarize students with the procedure for marking the lecture "Atoms," and have students read and mark the lecture. Then have students complete the notetaking format.

4-12 Rewriting Notes

Explain why notes may have to be rewritten. Have students examine two different ways notes can be rewritten, and then tell which they prefer and why. Some students may prefer to use both or may suggest other ways notes can be rewritten.

4-13 Mastery Assessment and Reflection

Have students complete this assessment when you believe they have learned to use the notetaking strategy presented in this chapter. Review the results of the assessment with students. Provide additional instruction as needed.

Thinking about How I Take Notes

You take notes in class to have a written record of important information. Think about how you take notes when your teacher is giving information in class. Describe the things you do at each of the following stages of notetaking.

1. This is what I do to **GET READY** to take notes in class.

_____

_____

_____

_____

_____

_____

_____

2. This is what I do when I *TAKE* notes in class.

_____

_____

_____

_____

_____

_____

_____

3. This is what I do with my notes *AFTER* class.

_____

_____

_____

_____

_____

_____

_____

Reread what you wrote in 4-1 about how you take notes. Then listen as your teacher explains the three stages of notetaking. Circle Yes for each idea you listed in 4-1.

Get Ready Stage

Yes   Have notetaking materials ready.

Yes   Review notes from the last class.

Yes   Complete reading assignment.

Take Notes Stage

Yes   Listen for signal words and statements.

Yes   Write using abbreviations and symbols.

Yes   Write using the fewest words possible.

Yes   Listen for the teacher's lecture style.

Yes   Copy information presented visually.

Yes   Circle unknown words.

Yes   Underline anything you wrote but did not understand.

Yes   Leave space for missing information.

After Notes Stage

Yes   Have someone explain ideas you wrote but did not understand.

Yes   Look up the meanings of unknown words.

Yes   Compare notes with other students.

Yes   Rewrite notes as necessary.

Signal Words

During a lecture, your teacher often will use words to tell you that something is important to write in your notes. These words are called **signal words**. If you listen for signal words, you will be more likely to write down important information.

Here are some signal words used by teachers.

first   second   next   finally

Read the following lecture. The topic is "Losing Your Hair." As you read the lecture, see how these signal words call your attention to important information. Circle each of these signal words as you read the lecture.

Losing Your Hair

As people get older, they typically lose some of their hair. Men usually lose their hair at an earlier age than women. However, there are many bald women, just as there are bald men. People don't like to lose their hair because they think it makes them look older. There are several things that can be done to stop the loss of hair. The first thing most people try is to take better care of their hair by regular shampooing. There are many different types of shampoos available, many of which promise to stop the loss of hair. The second remedy is to massage the scalp regularly with a stiff brush or with one's fingers. When this doesn't help, the next thing people usually try is vitamin therapy. There are many different vitamins that are thought to encourage hair growth.

Finally, when all else fails, people go out and buy a wig or toupee. Both are used to cover part or all of the scalp. As you see, it is natural to lose hair, but there are things you can do to keep that "young look."

Write a paragraph on the following topic. Use signal words in your paragraph.

Topic: Taking Good Notes in Class

_____

_____

_____

_____

_____

Teachers often use **signal statements** to tell you that something is important to write in your notes. Teachers use signal statements like these:

> "Here is something you should know."
> "I wouldn't forget this point, if I were you."
> "Remember this."
> "This is particularly important."
> "There are five things you have to know."

Read the following lecture. The topic is "The Roman Army." As you read the lecture, look for signal statements that call your attention to important information. Underline each signal statement as you read the lecture.

The Roman Army

The expansion of Rome was made possible in part by the courage and skill of its soldiers. Be sure to remember that the Roman army became a match for any army in the Western world. The Roman army was made up mostly of foot soldiers. In early times, the soldiers were organized into groups of 8,000 called phalanxes. Make sure that you know that a phalanx was a group of soldiers massed together with shields joined and spears overlapping. Later the army replaced phalanxes with legions. A legion was made up of 3,600 men. Write in your notes that the legion was much more effective in battle than a phalanx. Roman soldiers were tough, loyal, practical men. The major thing to know is that they could handle just about any task, from repairing weapons to sewing their own clothes. They had to obey rules or face very severe punishment. The most important point is that because of its great army, Rome took over all of Italy. I am going to expect you to know that when the Roman army began to weaken, Rome began to lose its control of Italy.

Make a list of signal statements you use to tell that something is important. Signal statements I use:

_____

_____

_____

_____

Abbreviating Words

4-5

A good way to increase your notetaking speed is to abbreviate words. An **abbreviation** is a short way of writing something. Here are some words and the abbreviations that can be used to write them.

Word	Abbreviation
psychology	psy
English	Eng
month	mo
vocabulary	vocab

Word	Abbreviation
medicine	med
diameter	dia
year	yr
Florida	Fl

Here are some words you may have to write when taking notes. For each word, write an abbreviation. You must be able to recognize the word from your abbreviation.

November   _____

amendment   _____

general   _____

Africa   _____

William   _____

science   _____

interest   _____

library   _____

kidney   _____

history   _____

computer   _____

geography   _____

Abbreviating Statements

You can also increase your notetaking speed by **abbreviating statements**. For example, you can abbreviate *grade point average* as *gpa*, or *home computer* as *ho comp*.

You can also abbreviate the names of organizations or titles. For example, *Federal Bureau of Investigation* is commonly abbreviated *FBI*. The *chief executive officer* of a company is commonly abbreviated *CEO*.

Create an abbreviation for each of the following:

Organization of American States _____

Republic of China _____

mathematics teacher _____

football coach _____

weekly assignment _____

National Aeronautics and Space Agency _____

North Atlantic Treaty Organization _____

shopping list _____

longitude and latitude _____

Saturday afternoon and evening _____

television program _____

World Wide Web _____

pencil and paper _____

Using Symbols

Another way to increase your notetaking speed is to **use symbols** for words or terms. Here are some common words and terms and their symbols.

%	percent	&	and	+	plus
@	at	#	number	$	money
=	equals, equal to	?	question	–	minus
×	multiply	∴	therefore	∵	because
÷	divided by	≠	not equal to	\	difference
>	greater than	<	less than	‖	parallel
⊥	perpendicular	∠	angle	°	degree
′	minute	″	second	¢	cent

Use what you know about abbreviations and symbols to rewrite these sentences.

1. The question before the United States Supreme Court is concerned with ensuring that justice for one group of people is not greater than justice for another group of people.

   _____

   _____

   _____

2. Five percent of one hundred dollars is less than five percent of one thousand dollars.

   _____

   _____

   _____

3. Sam completed the race in less than 25 minutes, 13 seconds, because the track had few angle turns.

   _____

   _____

   _____

4. The difference between parallel lines and perpendicular lines is that parallel lines go in the same direction, whereas perpendicular lines intersect or form right angles.

   _____

   _____

   _____

Using the Fewest Words

When you take notes, try to **use the fewest words** while keeping the important ideas. For example, instead of, "As airs cools, it loses its ability to hold water vapor," you could write, "Cool air holds less water vapor."

For each sentence below, rewrite the sentence in a shorter form.

1. As we have noted, the Constitution gives to each branch of the government its own distinct field of governmental authority: legislative, executive, and judicial.

   _____

   _____

   _____

2. The weight at which you look and feel most comfortable is your "ideal" weight or the healthiest weight for your body.

   _____

   _____

   _____

3. Any water used for drinking purposes not only must be free of salt but also should be free of foreign matter.

   _____

   _____

   _____

4. The common cold is really a group of symptoms and signs caused by a variety of viruses.

   _____

   _____

   _____

5. Each of the American colonies was born out of a particular set of circumstances, and so each had its own character.

   _____

   _____

Two Common Lecture Styles

Teachers lecture using different styles. Identifying the lecture style used by a teacher will help you organize the way you listen and take notes. Here is how to identify two common lecture styles used by teachers.

You will know that the Topic–Subtopic–Detail (TSD) lecture style is being used when a teacher:

1. Begins by presenting a topic for the lecture.
2. Follows by presenting the first subtopic.
3. Continues with a list of details that goes with the first subtopic.
4. Goes on to the next subtopic and its details.
5. Continues until all subtopics and details are presented.

You will know that the Question–Answer–Detail (QAD) lecture style is being used when a teacher:

1. Begins by presenting a topic for the lecture.
2. Follows by asking a question about the topic.
3. Continues by providing an answer to the question.
4. The teacher may add additional details.
5. Goes on to ask and answer another question.
6. Continues until all questions have been presented and answered.

What is the difference between the TSD and QAD lecture styles?

_____

_____

_____

_____

_____

_____

_____

_____

_____

_____

Read the following shortened lecture. It is organized in the Topic–Subtopic–Detail (TSD) lecture style.

As you read:

- Draw [ ] around the topic.
- Draw a <u>single line</u> under each subtopic.
- Draw ( ) around details that go with a subtopic.

Sources of Conflict

The Civil War between the northern and southern states did not begin until 1861. However, as early as the period of 1816–1823 there were several sources of conflict between the North and South. One had to do with the building of a national road from east to west across what was then the United States. The southern states were more interested in developing resources in their states than expanding across the continent. Another problem had to do with tariffs on imported goods. The northern states had factories that were able to manufacture the products they needed. This was not true in the agricultural South. The South had to import goods that were manufactured elsewhere. In many cases they bought manufactured goods from other countries. The tariff on imported goods made these products very expensive. Third, much of the taxes paid by the southern states to the United States government was used by the government to increase industrial growth in the northern states. Would you like to pay taxes that helped someone else and not yourself? I wouldn't. Finally, the Bank of the United States was taking away business from private banks in the South. The southern states needed their banks to build factories. When you consider these sources of conflict, the outbreak of the Civil War is not surprising.

This is the notetaking format to use when you recognize that your teacher is following the TSD lecture style.

Complete this notetaking format for the lecture about "Sources of Conflict."

Sources of Conflict

Topic: _____

First subtopic: _____

Detail(s): _____

_____

_____

_____

Second subtopic: _____

Detail(s): _____

_____

_____

_____

Third subtopic: _____

Detail(s): _____

_____

_____

_____

Fourth subtopic: _____

Detail(s): _____

_____

_____

_____

Read the following shortened lecture. It is organized in the Question–Answer–Detail (QAD) lecture style.

As you read:

- Draw [ ] around the topic.
- Draw a <u>single line</u> under each question.
- Draw a <u>double line</u> under the answer to each question.
- Draw ( ) around details that go with an answer.

Atoms

Here is a way to think about atoms. Think about an element such as gold being cut into pieces that are smaller and smaller. At a certain point the pieces become too small to be seen even with a microscope. Now just imagine that you keep doing this cutting until you end up with the smallest piece of matter that still has the chemical properties of gold. What do you call this piece of matter? It is called an atom. An atom is defined as the smallest part of an element that has the chemical properties of that element. All matter is made of atoms. Who do you think first thought about atoms? It wasn't Einstein. It was long before his time. It was the ancient Greeks who first hypothesized about the existence of atoms. It wasn't until the early 1800s that scientists began to get a good understanding of atoms. Does anyone here know the name of the scientist who developed an atomic theory of matter that helped to explain what atoms are? He was English. His name was John Dalton, and his theory motivated other scientists to learn more about atoms.

This is the notetaking format to use when you recognize that your teacher is following the QAD lecture style.

Complete this notetaking format for the lecture about "Atoms."

Atoms

Topic: _____

First question: _____

Answer: _____

Detail(s): _____

_____

_____

_____

Second question: _____

Answer: _____

Detail(s): _____

_____

_____

_____

Third question: _____

Answer: _____

Detail(s): _____

_____

_____

_____

Rewriting Notes

Sometimes the notes you take when listening to a lecture are not as complete as you would like. When this is the case, compare your notes with those of other students or ask your teacher questions. Add the information you learn to make your notes more complete. After you have added the new information, you may want to rewrite your notes. Here are two ways to do this.

A student's original notes from "Sources of Conflict."

> Confl N & S 1816-1823. 1. bld nat road E 2 W U.S.
> 2. tariffs imports. S had to import more th N. Made prod expens.
> 3. taxes pd by south used in N.   4. US Bank hurt bus S banks.

Rewritten Word Notes

There were sources of conflict between the N & S 1816-23 that led to the civil war.

1. N wanted to build national road from east to west across what was then the U.S. S interested in developing own area—not interested in expanding U.S.

2. N wanted tariffs on imports so goods made in the U.S. would be cheaper than imports. a. Not a prob for N bec they had fact to make products they needed. b. S mostly farms with few factories. Had to import most manufactured goods. Tariff added to the cost of goods.

3. Much of taxes paid by S used to develop industries in N.

4. Bank of US (in N) took business away from S banks. S need the money to finance its industrial growth.

Rewritten Graphic Notes

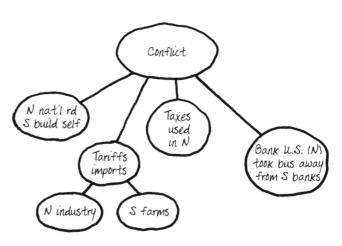

Which way would you like to rewrite your notes? Why?

_____

_____

_____

Mastery Assessment and Reflection

Show what you have learned about taking notes in class.

Get Ready Stage   Write a paragraph that tells how a good notetaker gets ready to take notes before a class begins.

_____

_____

_____

Take Notes Stage   Read the words in the box. Then write a paragraph that tells what a good note-taker does when taking notes during a class.

symbols   signal words   lecture style
statements   abbreviations   fewest words
don't understand   visual information
missing information   unknown words

_____

_____

_____

_____

After Notes Stage   Write a paragraph that tells what a good notetaker does with notes after a class.

_____

_____

_____

_____

Reflection   How does taking good notes in class make you a better student?

_____

_____

4-1 Student responses will vary.

4-2 Student responses will vary.

4-3 Signal words students should circle are: first, second, next, finally. Paragraphs written by students will vary in content but should include signal words.

4-4 Signal statements students should underline are:

"Be sure to remember"   "The major thing to know"

"Make sure that you know"   "The most important point"

"Write in your notes"   "I am going to expect you to know"

Signal statements students write will vary.

4-5 Student responses will vary.

4-6 Student responses will vary.

4-7 Student responses will vary.

4-8 Student responses will vary.

4-9 Student responses should bring out that the TSD style begins with a topic, followed by subtopics and details, while the ASD style begins with a question, followed by an answer and details.

4-10

[Sources of Conflict]

The Civil War between the northern and southern states did not begin until 1861. However, as early as the period of 1816–1823 there were [several sources of conflict] between the North and South. One had to do with the building of a national road from east to west across what was then the United States. The southern states were more interested in developing resources in their states than expanding across the continent. Another problem had to do with tariffs on imported goods. The (northern states had factories that were able to manufacture the products they needed). This was not true in the agricultural South. The (South had to import goods that were manufactured elsewhere.) In many cases they bought manufactured goods from other countries. The tariff on imported goods made these products very expensive. Third, much of the taxes paid by the southern states to the United States government was used by the government to increase industrial growth in the northern states. Would you like to pay taxes that helped someone else and not yourself? I wouldn't. Finally, the Bank of the United States was (taking away business from private banks) in the South. The (southern states needed their banks to build factories.) When you consider these sources of conflict, the outbreak of the Civil War is not surprising.

Sources of Conflict

Topic:	sources of conflict
First Subtopic:	building of a national road
Details:	none
Second Subtopic:	tariffs on imported goods
Details:	northern states manufactured products they needed
	South had to import goods manufactured elsewhere

Third Subtopic:	taxes
Details:	none
Fourth Subtopic:	Bank of the United States
Details:	took business away from private banks
	South needed banks to build factories

4-11

[Atoms]

Here is a way to think about [atoms]. Think about an element such as gold being cut into pieces that are smaller and smaller. At a certain point the pieces become too small to be seen even with a microscope. Now just imagine that you keep doing this cutting until you end up with the smallest piece of matter that still has the chemical properties of gold. <u>What do you call this piece of matter?</u> It is called an <u>atom</u>. An atom is defined as the (smallest part of an element) that (has the chemical properties of that element.) (All matter is made of atoms.) <u>Who do you think first thought about atoms?</u> It wasn't Einstein. It was long before his time. It was the <u>ancient Greeks</u> who first hypothesized about the existence of atoms. It wasn't until the early 1800s that scientists began to get a good understanding of atoms. <u>Does anyone here know the name of the scientist who developed an atomic theory of matter that helped to explain what atoms are?</u> (He was English.) His name was <u>John Dalton,</u> and his theory (motivated other scientists) to learn more about atoms.

Atoms	
Topic:	atoms
First Question:	What do you call this piece of matter?
Answer:	atom
Details:	the smallest part of an element
	has the chemical properties of that element
	all matter is made of atoms
Second Question:	Who first thought about atoms?
Answer:	ancient Greeks
Details:	none
Third Question:	What was the name of the scientist who developed a theory to explain what atoms were?
Answer:	John Dalton
Details:	English
	motivated other scientists to learn about atoms

4-12 Student responses will vary.

4-13 Student responses will vary but should reflect the information presented in the chapter.

Reflection Responses will vary but should reveal insights into how the student has become a better learner.

CHAPTER FIVE

Making Good Use of Study Time and Space

TITLES OF REPRODUCIBLE ACTIVITIES

USING THE REPRODUCIBLE ACTIVITIES

After you have distributed a reproducible activity, here are suggestions for its use. Define any terms and clarify any concepts students do not know. Feel free to add further information, illustrations, or examples. Wherever possible, relate the activity to actual subject-area assignments.

5-1 A Strategy for Making Good Use of Study Time

Lead students in a discussion of the importance of using time effectively. Tell them that successful students schedule and manage their time to complete their schoolwork and responsibilities, yet still have some time for fun. Explain each of the three steps in the strategy for making good use of study time. Have students write statements about what should be done in each step.

5-2 Learning about a Term Calendar
5-3 Term Calendar

Discuss the purposes of a term calendar. Review the three things students should do to use a term calendar. Have students list on 5-2 their school assignments, school activities, and out-of-school activities for the term. Tell students to include dates. Distribute copies of 5-3 for each month of the term. Have students enter dates and then record information from 5-2 on 5-3.

5-4 Learning about a Weekly Planner
5-5 Weekly Planner

Discuss the purposes of a weekly planner. Review the three things students should do to prepare a weekly planner. Have students complete the lists in 5-4 for the coming week. Distribute copies of 5-5. Have students record information from 5-4 on 5-5. Repeat this procedure for each week.

5-6 Learning about a Daily Planner
5-7 Daily Planner

Discuss the purposes of a daily planner. Review the five things students do to prepare a daily planner. Have students complete the lists in 5-6 for the next day. Distribute copies of 5-7. Have students record information from 5-6 on 5-7. Remind students to complete a daily planner each evening before a school day.

5-8 Checking My Study Habits

Lead students in a discussion of the importance of good study habits. Then have students complete 5-8.

5-9 Improving My Study Habits

Have students write any study habits for which they checked "No" on 5-8. For each habit, have them write what they will do to improve it. Have students share with the class what they will do.

5-10 Checking My Study Place

Discuss with students the importance of having a good place to study. Then have students complete 5-10.

5-11 Improving My Study Place

Have students write any study-place feature for which they checked "No" on 5-10. For each study-place feature included, have them write what they will do to improve it. Have students share with the class what they will do.

5-12 Mastery Assessment and Reflection

Have students complete this assessment when you feel they have learned about good use of time and space and good study habits. Review the results of the assessment with the students. Provide additional instruction as needed.

A Strategy for Making Good Use of Study Time

 5-1

Have you ever felt as though you have too much schoolwork to do and not enough time to do it? You cannot do anything to change the amount of schoolwork you have. That is up to your teachers. But you can change the way in which you use the time you have.

Here is a three-step strategy you can employ to make good use of your study time:

Step 1   Prepare a **term calendar**. This calendar should show all your important school and out-of-school activities and assignments for a term. Prepare a term calendar at the beginning of each school term. Add new items to your calendar as the term goes on.

Step 2   Prepare a **weekly planner**. This planner should show your school and out-of-school activities and assignments for a week. Prepare a weekly planner at the beginning of each school week. Add new items as the week goes on.

Step 3   Prepare a **daily planner**. This planner should show what you must do each day and when you plan to do it. Prepare a daily planner each evening for the next school day.

Write a statement that tells what you must do for each step in the strategy for making good use of your study time.

1. _____

_____

_____

_____

2. _____

_____

_____

_____

3. _____

_____

_____

_____

Learning about a Term Calendar

To do all the things you want to do each term, you need to schedule your time. A **term calendar** will remind you when you need to start and finish important school and out-of-school activities. It will help you plan your time so you can get done everything you must do. A term calendar helps you to organize your school and out-of-school activities for an entire term. Here is how to use a term calendar:

> 1. Ask each of your teachers for a list of assignments and due dates. Write them on your term calendar.
> 2. Get a list of the school activities for the current term and their dates. Write them on your term calendar.
> 3. Make a list of the out-of-school activities in which you plan to be involved. These include such things as attending sporting events, going to club meetings, and going on family trips. Write the activities and dates on your term calendar.

List the school assignments you know you will have this term. Also write the due dates.

_____

_____

_____

List the school activities you know you will be involved with this term. Also write the dates.

_____

_____

_____

List the out-of-school activities you know you will be involved with this term. Also write the dates.

_____

_____

_____

Finally, use these lists to complete the term calendar provided by your teacher. Each page in the term calendar is for one month of the term.

5-3

Name: _____

Month: _____

Monday	Tuesday	Wednesday	Thursday	Friday	Saturday	Sunday

Use a **weekly planner** to show in detail what you are planning to do during a school week. Here is how to prepare a weekly planner:

> Each Sunday evening:
> 1. Review your term calendar to see what you planned to do during the upcoming week. Enter this information into your weekly planner.
> 2. Review notes from your classes to see what else needs to be added to your weekly planner.
> 3. Think of the out-of-school activities you need to add to your weekly planner.

List items from your term calendar that you need to record on your weekly planner.

_____

_____

_____

_____

List items from your class notes you need to record on your weekly planner.

_____

_____

_____

_____

List out-of-school activities you need to record on your weekly planner.

_____

_____

_____

_____

Finally, use these lists to complete the weekly planner provided to you by your teacher.

Weekly Planner

NAME _____ WEEK OF _____

	MONDAY	TUESDAY	WEDNESDAY	THURSDAY	FRIDAY	SATURDAY	SUNDAY
8:00							
9:00							
10:00							
11:00							
12:00							
1:00							
2:00							
3:00							
AFTER SCHOOL							
EVENING							

Each evening before a school day, you should prepare a **daily planner**. The daily planner shows how you will use your time that day. Here is how to prepare a daily planner.

1. Review your weekly planner to see what you need to do tomorrow.
2. Review your class notes to see what you need to do tomorrow.
3. Review your daily planner for today to determine what you did not get done. Add these things to your daily planner for tomorrow.
4. For each thing you need to do tomorrow, decide how much time you need to do it.
5. Decide when you will do each thing. Write the thing you need to do in the appropriate time period in your daily planner.

List the things from your weekly planner that you need to do tomorrow. Next to each, tell how much time you need to do it.

_____

_____

_____

_____

List things from your class notes you know you need to do tomorrow. Next to each, tell how much time you need to do each thing.

_____

_____

_____

_____

List things you did not finish from today's daily planner that you will need to do tomorrow. Next to each, tell how much time you need to do each thing.

_____

_____

_____

_____

Finally, use these lists to complete the daily planner provided by your teacher.

Daily Planner

NAME _____ DAY/DATE _____

7:00 _____

8:00 _____

9:00 _____

10:00 _____

11:00 _____

12:00 _____

1:00 _____

2:00 _____

3:00 _____

4:00 _____

5:00 _____

6:00 _____

7:00 _____

8:00 _____

Checking My Study Habits

Read about each study habit. If it is something you do most of the time, place a ✔ under Yes. If not, place a ✔ under No.

My Study Habits	Yes	No
I have a planned study time.		
I tell my friends not to call me during my study time.		
I start working on time.		
I review my notes before beginning an assignment.		
I begin with the hardest assignment.		
I finish one assignment before going on to another.		
I take short breaks when I feel tired.		
I avoid daydreaming.		
I have a "study buddy" I can contact when I get stuck.		
I write down questions I will need to ask my teacher.		
I keep working on long-term assignments.		

Improving My Study Habits

Write down each study habit for which you checked "No" when completing 5-8. Then write a sentence that tells what you will do to improve each study habit.

Study habit to be improved: _____

What I will do to improve it: _____

_____

Study habit to be improved: _____

What I will do to improve it: _____

_____

Study habit to be improved: _____

What I will do to improve it: _____

_____

Study habit to be improved: _____

What I will do to improve it: _____

_____

Study habit to be improved: _____

What I will do to improve it: _____

_____

Study habit to be improved: _____

What I will do to improve it: _____

_____

Read each feature of a study place. If your study place has the feature, place a ✔ under Yes. If it does not, place a ✔ under No.

My Study Place	*Yes*	*No*
It is quiet.		
There are no things that take attention away from working.		
There is good light.		
The temperature is comfortable.		
There is a comfortable chair.		
It contains all needed work materials.		
It contains all needed reference sources.		
It contains a desk or table large enough to work at comfortably.		
It contains enough storage space.		
It can be used whenever needed.		

Improving My Study Place

Write down each feature for which you checked "No" when completing 5-10. Then write a sentence that tells what you will do to improve each study-place feature.

Feature that needs to be improved: _____

What I will do to improve it: _____

_____

_____

Feature that needs to be improved: _____

What I will do to improve it: _____

_____

_____

Feature that needs to be improved: _____

What I will do to improve it: _____

_____

_____

Feature that needs to be improved: _____

What I will do to improve it: _____

_____

_____

Feature that needs to be improved: _____

What I will do to improve it: _____

_____

_____

Mastery Assessment and Reflection

Directions Show what you have learned about study time, habits, and space by writing an answer for each of the following.

1. Why should you prepare a term calendar?

   _____

   _____

   _____

2. Weekly planner?

   _____

   _____

   _____

3. Daily planner?

   _____

   _____

   _____

4. How can checking your study habits help you become a better student?

   _____

   _____

   _____

5. How can checking your study place help you become a better student?

   _____

   _____

   _____

Reflection How does making good use of study time and space make you a better student?

_____

_____

5-1 1. Prepare a term calendar showing important things to do both in school and out of school for the term. 2. Prepare a weekly calendar showing in-school and out-of-school activities for a week. 3. Prepare a daily planner to show what must be done each day.

5-2 Responses will vary.

5-3 Entries will vary according to the information recorded on 5-2.

5-4 Responses will vary.

5-5 Entries will vary according to the information recorded on 5-4.

5-6 Responses will vary.

5-7 Entries will vary according to the information recorded on 5-6.

5-8 Responses will vary.

5-9 Entries will vary according to the information recorded on 5-8.

5-10 Responses will vary.

5-11 Entries will vary according to the information recorded on 5-10.

5-12 1. To have a long-range plan for organizing your in-school and out-of-school activities for the term. 2. To prepare for the upcoming week. 3. To show what you must do each day and when you plan to do it. 4. By identifying study habits that need to be improved. 5. By identifying study-place features that need to be improved.

Reflection Responses will vary but should reveal insights into how the student has become a better learner.

## CHAPTER 6

Preparing for and Taking Tests

TITLES OF REPRODUCIBLE ACTIVITIES

USING THE REPRODUCIBLE ACTIVITIES

After you have distributed a reproducible activity, here are suggestions for its use. Define any terms and clarify any concepts students do not know.

Feel free to add further information, illustrations, or examples. Wherever possible, relate the activity to actual subject-area assignments.

6-1 Preparing for Tests

Tell students that to do well on a test, they must be prepared. Introduce students to the five-step plan they should follow to be prepared to take a test. Have students complete the activity.

6-2 Five-Day Test Preparation Plan

Introduce the five-day test preparation plan and review what must be done on each day. If necessary, review with students how notes are taken from textbooks (Chapter Two) and in class (Chapter Four), and how remembering strategies are used to remember information (Chapter One). Have students complete the activity.

6-3 Using the DETER Strategy to Do Well on a Test

Introduce the acronym DETER as a strategy for taking a test. Remind students that just remembering information for a test is not sufficient to do well on a test. They must also know how to take a test. Have students complete the activity.

6-4 Learning about Multiple-Choice Test Items

Use the sample items to explain two types of multiple-choice items. Then have students use the *information* provided to write a multiple-choice item for each type.

6-5 What to Do When Taking Multiple-Choice Tests

Use the statements to explain to students what they should do when taking multiple-choice tests. Have students write notes in the space provided.

6-6 Practice Taking a Multiple-Choice Test

Review with students what they have learned about multiple-choice test items and taking multiple-choice tests. Then have students complete the test. Go over the answers with the students.

6-7 What to Do When Taking True/False Tests

Use the statements to explain to students what they should do when taking true/false tests. Have students write notes as needed.

6-8 Practice Taking a True/False Test

Review with students what they have learned about true/false tests. Then have students complete the test. Go over the answers with the students.

6-9 What to Do When Taking Matching Tests

Use the example of a matching test item to show one format in which matching test items appear. Explain other formats as appropriate for your students. For example, responses may be written next to words or terms in the first column, or there may be a different number of words and terms in each column.

Use the statements to explain to students what they should do when taking matching tests. Have students write notes as needed.

6-10 Practice Taking a Matching Test

Review with students what they have learned about taking matching tests. Then have students complete the two tests. Go over the answers with the students. The test items are based on commonly known information. If necessary, review the information before students take the test.

6-11 What to Do When Taking Completion Tests

Use the statements to explain to students what they should do when taking completion tests. Have students write notes as needed.

6-12 Practice Taking a Completion Test

Review with students what they have learned about taking completion tests. Then have students complete the test. Go over the answers with the students. The test items are based on commonly known information. If necessary, review the information before students take the test.

6-13 The QUOTE Strategy for Taking Essay Tests

Introduce QUOTE as a strategy for taking essay tests. Have students take notes as you explain each step in the strategy.

6-14 QUOTE: Question

Use the activity to explain the Question step in the QUOTE strategy for answering essay test items. Introduce the direction words *discuss, describe,* and *explain*. Have students place [   ] around direction words in the sample essay test items.

6-15 More Direction Words

Use this activity to familiarize students with additional direction words they will see in essay test items. Add additional information as needed. Have students select an appropriate direction word to complete each of the essay test items.

6-16 QUOTE: Underline

Use the activity to explain the Underline step in the QUOTE strategy for answering essay test items. For each item, have students bracket the direction word and underline the words that help them focus on the ideas to develop in their answer.

6-17 QUOTE: Organize/Write

Use the activity to explain the Organize/Write step in the QUOTE strategy for answering essay test items. Then review with students the procedures for writing one- and multiple-paragraph answers to essay test items. Finally, have students write an answer to the essay test item that concludes the activity.

6-18 QUOTE: Time

Use the activity to explain the Time step in the QUOTE strategy for answering essay test items. Review with students the procedure for deciding how much time should be spent answering each test item. Finally, have students answer the questions to show what they have learned about planning their time when taking an essay test.

6-19 QUOTE: Evaluate

Use the activity to explain the Evaluate step in the QUOTE strategy for answering essay test items. Review with students the items for evaluating the content, writing, and mechanics of answers to essay test items. Then have students use the items to evaluate the answer they wrote to the essay test item in 6-17. Finally, based on their responses of *yes* or *no* to the items in 6-19, have students write a statement that tells how they could improve the answer they wrote for the essay test item in 6-17.

6-20 Mastery Assessment and Reflection

Have students complete this assessment when you believe they have learned how to prepare for and take the different types of tests presented in this chapter. Review the results of the assessment with students. Provide additional instruction as needed.

Here are five steps you should follow to be prepared to take a test. You will get higher scores on your tests if you follow these steps.

1. To do well on a test, you must begin to prepare early. Schedule your time so you have enough time to study for the test. Do not wait until the night before a test to begin studying. You will learn how to use a five-day test preparation plan in Activity 6-2.
2. Learn what the test will cover. Ask your teacher:
   - What will be covered on the test?
   - What will not be covered on the test?
3. Ask your teacher what type of test will be given: multiple choice, true/false, matching, completion, essay.
4. Gather the information you need to study from your textbook notes, class notes, and teacher handouts. Ask your teacher to explain anything you do not understand.
5. Use the remembering strategies taught in Chapter One to help you remember the information you are studying.

Write a sentence that tells about each step you should follow to be prepared to take a test:

1. _____

_____

_____

2. _____

_____

_____

3. _____

_____

_____

4. _____

_____

_____

5. _____

_____

_____

You should begin studying for a test five days before the test. Follow this five-day plan to get a high score on your tests. Each day gets you more ready for the test. Here is what you should do on each of the five days:

Day 5   Read your textbook notes and class notes. Also look at any handouts your teacher has given you. Highlight the information in your notes and handouts that you must know and remember for the test.

Day 4   Use the remembering strategies taught in Chapter One to help you remember the information you identified on Day 5.

Day 3   Rewrite the information in a brief form using the fewest words you can. Use abbreviations and symbols wherever possible. Use the remembering strategies to review your rewritten notes at least twice on this day.

Day 2   Think of the questions your teacher might ask on the test. Write each question and its answer.

Day 1   This is the day you take your test. Review your rewritten notes from Day 3. Also review the questions and answers you prepared on Day 2. You can do this while eating breakfast or while riding to school. Just before the test, go over any information you are having difficulty remembering.

Think about what you should do each day of the five-day test preparation plan. For each day, write a sentence that tells what you will do on that day.

Day 5 _____

_____

Day 4 _____

_____

Day 3 _____

_____

Day 2 _____

_____

Day 1 _____

_____

Once you have learned the information, you are ready to take the test. The **DETER** strategy can help you get high scores on your test. Here are the five test-taking steps the acronym **DETER** will help you remember.

D   Read the test **Directions** carefully. Ask your teacher to explain any part of the directions you do not understand.

E   **Examine** the entire test to see how much you have to do. Do this right after you have read and understood the test directions.

T   Decide how much **Time** you should spend answering each item on the test. See how many items are on the test and how many points each item is worth. Spend the most time answering the items that count the most points.

E   Begin by answering the items that are **Easiest** for you. Then answer as many of the remaining items as you can. Be sure to answer all the items if there is no penalty for wrong answers.

R   If you finish the test before time is up, **Review** your answers to make sure they are accurate and complete. Then you are ready to hand in your test.

Write a sentence that tells what each letter of the acronym **DETER** reminds you to do:

D _____

_____

E _____

_____

T _____

_____

E _____

_____

R _____

_____

Here are two types of multiple-choice test items.

The first type of multiple-choice item has a question followed by answer choices. You have to identify the answer choice that correctly answers the question. Look at the example:

> Which holiday is observed to honor American soldiers killed during wars?
> a. Labor Day
> b. Presidents' Day
> c. Memorial Day
> d. Independence Day

The second type of multiple-choice item has an incomplete statement followed by answer choices. You have to identify the answer choice that correctly completes the statement. Look at the two examples:

> On the last Monday in May, _____ is observed to honor American soldiers killed during wars.
> a. Labor Day
> b. Presidents' Day
> c. Memorial Day
> d. Independence Day

> American soldiers killed during wars are honored on _____ .
> a. Labor Day
> b. Presidents' Day
> c. Memorial Day
> d. Independence Day

Use the following information to write a multiple-choice item for each type you just learned. Do this on your own paper.

Information   There are 50 states in the United States.

Here are some things you should do to choose the correct answer for a multiple-choice item. Add information to each as your teacher discusses it with you.

- Read the question or statement and underline key words such as *not, all, some, except*. These words can give you clues to the correct answer.

  _____

  _____

- Read the question or statement along with each answer choice to help you decide which choice is correct.

  _____

  _____

- Once you decide that an answer choice is incorrect, cross out the answer choice by drawing a line through it.

  _____

  _____

- If you crossed out all the answer choices except one, select as your answer the choice you did not cross out.

  _____

  _____

- If you are left with more than one answer choice that you did not cross out, reread the question or statement with the remaining answer choices and choose the best answer.

  _____

  _____

- Answer all items unless there is a penalty for incorrect answers.

  _____

  _____

- Check your answers to make certain they are correct.

  _____

  _____

- Change an answer only if you are sure it is incorrect.

  _____

  _____

Practice Taking a Multiple-Choice Test

Take this multiple-choice test to show what you have learned. There is no penalty for incorrect answers. Each correct answer is worth one point. You will have five minutes to complete the test.

Directions   For each item, circle the letter of the correct answer.

1. Change your answer only when you are sure it is
   a. too long.
   b. too short.
   c. correct.
   d. incorrect.

2. What should you do when you decide an answer choice is incorrect?
   a. Reread the answer choice.
   b. Cross out the answer choice.
   c. Rewrite the answer choice.
   d. Guess at the answer.

3. Do not answer an item about whose answer you are unsure, unless
   a. you do not understand the item.
   b. you cannot read some of the words.
   c. there is no penalty for incorrect answers.
   d. it is a hard item.

4. What should you do to key words in an item?
   a. Cross them out.
   b. Underline them.
   c. Ignore them.
   d. Rewrite them.

5. Read the _____ with each answer choice to decide which answer is correct.
   a. key words
   b. question or statement
   c. first word in an item
   d. last word in an item

Check your answers as your teacher goes over them with you. Count your number correct and use this chart to see how you did.

5 items correct	=	Excellent
4 items correct	=	Good
0–3 items correct	=	Review the information in 6-4 and 6-5.

Here are some things you should do to choose the correct answer for a true/false item. Add information to each as your teacher discusses it with you.

- Choose **TRUE** unless you are sure that a statement is **FALSE**.
- For a statement to be **TRUE,** everything about the statement must be **TRUE**. For example, the following statement is **TRUE** because everything about it is **TRUE**.

> Maine, Ohio, and California are states that are a part of the United States.

This statement is **TRUE** because Maine, Ohio, and California are states that are part of the United States.

Now look at this statement:

> New York, Florida, and England are states that are part of the United States.

This statement is **FALSE** because not all parts of the statement are **TRUE**. England is a country. It is not a state that is part of the United States.

- Be careful when a statement has a negative such as *not, do not,* or *in* (infrequent) and *un* (unfriendly). A negative can completely change the meaning of a statement. For example, compare:

1. George Washington was the first president of the United States.
2. George Washington was not the first president of the United States.

or

1. Twelve months is a complete year.
2. Twelve months is an incomplete year.

- If a statement has two negatives, cross out both negatives. This will make it easier for you to understand the statement. For example, look at the two statements that follow. The second statement is easier to understand because the two negatives have been crossed out.

1. You will not get good grades if you do not study.
2. You will ~~not~~ get good grades if you ~~do not~~ study.

- Absolute statements are usually **FALSE**. Absolute statements include such terms as *all, every, never, no.*

  For example, this statement is **FALSE** because the word *all* makes it an absolute statement.

  All presidents of the United States were born in Virginia.

- Qualified statements are usually **TRUE**. Qualified statements include such terms as *some, most, sometimes, rarely.*

  For example, this statement is **TRUE** because the word *some* makes it a qualified statement.

  Some presidents of the United States were born in Virginia.

- If you are not sure about an item, take a guess at the answer, unless there is a penalty for guessing.

Take this sample true/false test to show what you have learned. There is no penalty for incorrect answers. Each correct answer is worth one point. You will have five minutes to complete the test.

Directions   Circle **TRUE** or **FALSE** for each of the following.

TRUE   FALSE   **1.** A negative can completely change the meaning of a statement.

TRUE   FALSE   **2.** Absolute statements are usually false.

TRUE   FALSE   **3.** If any part of a statement is false, then the statement is false.

TRUE   FALSE   **4.** If you are not certain that a statement is false, consider it false.

TRUE   FALSE   **5.** Qualified statements are usually false.

TRUE   FALSE   **6.** If a statement has two negatives, you should cross out one of the negatives.

TRUE   FALSE   **7.** If there is a penalty for incorrect answers, guess on any item for which you are unsure whether the statement is true or false.

Check your answers as your teacher goes over them with you. Count your number correct and use this chart to see how you did.

7 items correct	=	Excellent
5 or 6 items correct	=	Good
0–4 items correct	=	Review the information in 6-7.

Look at the matching test item. Matching test items require that you match words or terms in one column with words or terms in a second column. In the item shown, countries in the first column are matched with continents in the second column. The answers are provided to show you how this is done.

Country		*Continent*	
1. Canada	A.	_2_	Europe
2. France	B.	_4_	South America
3. China	C.	_3_	Asia
4. Brazil	D.	_1_	North America

Here are things to do when taking a matching test. Add information to each as your teacher explains it to you.

- Read all the items in both columns before making any matches.

_____

_____

_____

- Start by making the matches about which you are sure.

_____

_____

_____

- Cross out items in both columns as you make matches.

_____

_____

_____

- Make your best guess for remaining items, unless there is a penalty for incorrect answers.

_____

_____

_____

Practice Taking a Matching Test

Here are two matching tests. Use what you have learned about taking matching tests as you take each test. There is no penalty for incorrect answers. Your teacher will go over the answers with you.

Directions for Test One   Write the number for each person next to the thing for which they are famous.

1. Thomas Edison

2. Christopher Columbus

3. Neil Armstrong

4. George Washington

5. Walt Disney

A. _____   first president of the United States

B. _____   creator of Mickey Mouse

C. _____   first man to walk on the moon

D. _____   discovered America

E. _____   inventor of electric lightbulb

Directions for Test Two   For each body part write the letter that tells what that body part does.

_____ 1. hand

_____ 2. heart

_____ 3. stomach

_____ 4. eye

_____ 5. ear

A. sees things

B. pumps blood

C. hears sounds

D. digests food

E. picks up objects

Each item on a completion test has a part missing. The missing part is indicated with a line. You must write the missing part on the line.

Here are examples of completion test items with the missing part in different places. Answers are written to show you how they look when the item is answered.

1. When one country brings in a product that was made in another country, it is said to _import_ that product.

2. _Denver_ is the capital of Colorado and is its largest city.

3. The Gulf of _Mexico_ is bordered by the southern coast of the United States and the eastern coast of Mexico.

Here are things to do when taking a matching test. Add information to each as your teacher discusses it with you.

• Read the item and think about what is missing.

_____

_____

• Write an answer that logically completes the item.

_____

_____

• Be sure your answer fits the item grammatically.

_____

_____

• Use the length of the blank line as a clue to the length of the answer, unless the length of the blank line is the same for every item.

_____

_____

• After you write your answer on the blank line, read the entire item to make sure your answer makes sense.

_____

_____

6-12

Use what you have learned about taking completion tests as you take this test. There is no penalty for incorrect answers. Your teacher will go over the answers with you.

Directions Complete each item by writing the missing part on the blank line.

1. Red, white, and _____ are colors in the American flag.

2. There are _____ states in the United States.

3. A penny, nickel, dime, and half _____ are coins.

4. Mammals make milk to _____ their young.

5. The largest ocean in the world is the _____ Ocean.

6. _____ Jefferson was one of the signers of the Declaration of Independence.

7. The first ten amendments to the Constitution are called the _____ of Rights.

8. Coal, oil, and natural gas are fossil _____ .

9. When taking a completion test, be sure your answer _____ fits the statement.

10. After you write an answer to a completion test item, read the entire item to make sure your _____ makes sense.

QUOTE is a strategy that will help you to do well when taking essay tests. Each letter in the acronym stands for one of the five steps in **QUOTE**. Write more information about each step as your teacher explains it to you.

Question is the first step. Here you ask, "What is the direction word in the test item?" A direction word tells you what you must do to answer the item. Examples of direction words are *discuss, describe, explain.*

_____

_____

_____

Underline is the second step. Underline the words that help you focus on the ideas you will develop in your answer.

_____

_____

_____

Organize/Write is the third step. Organize the facts and write your answer.

_____

_____

_____

Time is the fourth step. Decide how much time you should spend answering each item.

_____

_____

_____

Evaluate is the fifth and final step. Evaluate the content and organization of what you wrote. Also evaluate your writing mechanics.

_____

_____

_____

Question is the first step you should apply in the **QUOTE** strategy for answering essay test items. Ask: "What is the direction word in the test item?" Identify and bracket [ ] the direction word. For example, look at how the direction word was bracketed in this essay test item.

> The government of the United States has three branches: executive, judicial, and legislative. [Describe] the executive branch.

Here are three direction words often used in essay test items. Read to find what each tells you to do.

> **Discuss** tells you to give reasons behind points of view.
> **Describe** tells you to present a detailed picture of something in words.
> **Explain** tells you to give the reason for something.

Bracket [   ] the direction word in each of these essay test items.

1. The Revolutionary War was the war for independence fought in the late 1700s by the American colonies against England. Explain why the colonies went to war.

2. Describe the role of George Washington as president of the United States.

3. Discuss the Democratic party's approach to the problem of poverty.

4. Explain the process by which plants absorb carbon dioxide and give off oxygen.

5. Briefly describe how gravity affects your life.

6. Many people are concerned about our environment. Discuss why many people want cars and trucks that burn a cleaner fuel.

Here are more direction words used in essay test items. Read what each direction word tells you to do. Write more information about each direction word as your teacher tells you more about it.

List:	Present information in some order.
Trace:	State a series of events in logical order.
Relate:	Show how two or more things are related.
Diagram:	Create a visual representation to show something.
Compare:	Tell how two or more things are alike and different.
Criticize:	Make positive and negative comments about something.
Evaluate:	Judge the merits of something using certain criteria.
Summarize:	State the major points about something.

Each of these essay test items is missing a direction word. Choose one of the direction words to complete each.

1. _____ the major ideas of the Democratic party and the Republican party.

2. John F. Kennedy was a popular president of the United States. _____ his performance as president.

3. The Civil War was fought between the northern states and the southern states. _____ the events that led to this war.

4. _____ the facts you know about the life of Helen Keller.

QUOTE: *Underline*

Underline is the second step you should apply in the **QUOTE** strategy for answering essay test items. After you have bracketed [   ] the direction word, underline the words that help you focus on the ideas to develop in your answer. The example shows you how to do this.

> The Great Depression was the worst economic period in American history. [Explain] <u>why the Great Depression happened</u> when it did.

For each essay test item, bracket the direction words and underline the words that help you focus on the ideas to develop in your answer.

1. Exercise should be an important part of everyone's life. Describe how exercise can help you to lead a healthy and satisfying life.

2. Controversy still exists about whether the United States was right to fight a war in Vietnam. Trace the events that led to our involvement in the Vietnam War.

3. The Constitution of the United States is the document that established the national government of the United States. Explain what the Founding Fathers tried to accomplish when they wrote this important document.

4. Communism remains a major economic and political system in many parts of the world. Compare the communist and democratic forms of government with respect to election of leaders.

5. Discuss the major positions taken by President George W. Bush as he campaigned to be elected in 2000.

Organize/Write is the third step in the **QUOTE** strategy. This is what you should do for this step:

1. Look at or write the words you underlined in the essay test item.
2. Write the facts that are related to the words you underlined.
3. Organize the facts by creating a graphic organizer.
4. Using the graphic organizer as a guide, write your answer.

Here is how to write a one-paragraph answer to an essay test item:

- Begin with an introductory sentence that contains your main point.
- Follow this sentence with sentences that support your point.
- End your answer with a sentence that states your conclusion.

Here is what to do when writing an answer that has more than one paragraph:

- Begin with an introductory paragraph that contains your main point.
- Follow with additional paragraphs, each of which has supporting points.
- End with a paragraph in which you state your conclusion.

Use what you have learned in the **Organize/Write** step to write an answer for the following essay-test item.

Describe what you have learned to do on each day when using the Five-Day Test Preparation Plan.

_____

_____

_____

_____

_____

_____

_____

_____

_____

_____

Time is the fourth step in the **QUOTE** strategy. For this step you must decide how much time to spend answering each item. Here is what you should do to decide how much time to spend answering each item:

- Determine the total time you have to complete the test.
- Consider how many points each item is worth. Plan to use more time for the items that count for the most points.
- Write in front of each item the amount of time you plan to use answering the item.
- Make sure that the time you plan for answering all items is not greater than the total time you have to take the test. If the time you planned is greater than the total time, revise your plan.

Pretend that you are about to take an essay test that has four items. The test counts for 100 points. The first item is worth 40 points. Each of the other three items is worth 20 points. You have 60 minutes to take the test.

1. What is the total time you have to take the test? _____

2. For which item should you use the most time? _____

3. Write the amount of time you plan to use for each item:

    Item 1 _____

    Item 2 _____

    Item 3 _____

    Item 4 _____

4. Add the amounts to find the total time you planned to use answering the four items. Write that amount here. _____

5. Is your total planned time greater than the total time you have to take the test? _____

6. What should you do if your planned time is greater than the time allowed to take the test?

    _____

    _____

    _____

    _____

Evaluate is the final step in the **QUOTE** strategy.

Evaluate the essay test answer you wrote in 6-17 by circling YES or NO for each of the following statements.

Content

I answered all parts of the item.	YES	NO
I included all the relevant facts.	YES	NO
All my facts are accurate.	YES	NO

Writing

My answer begins with an introduction.	YES	NO
My answer has supporting points.	YES	NO
My answer ends with a conclusion.	YES	NO

Mechanics

My handwriting is legible.	YES	NO
I spelled all words correctly.	YES	NO
I used correct punctuation.	YES	NO
I used correct grammar.	YES	NO

What can you do to improve the answer you wrote for the essay item in 6-17?

_____

_____

_____

_____

_____

_____

_____

Mastery Assessment and Reflection

Show what you have learned about preparing for and taking different types of tests by answering each of the following:

1. **Explain** the five things you should do to prepare for tests.

   _____

   _____

2. **List** the steps in the five-day test preparation plan.

   _____

   _____

3. **Summarize** what you should do when taking each of the following types of tests:

   Multiple-Choice _____

   _____

   True/False _____

   _____

   Matching _____

   _____

   Completion _____

   _____

4. Write what each letter in the **QUOTE** strategy reminds you to do when taking an essay test.

   _____

   _____

Reflection How has learning to prepare for tests and taking different types of tests made you a better student?

_____

_____

_____

ANSWER KEY FOR CHAPTER SIX

6-1 1. Begin to prepare early.   2. Ask the teacher what the test will cover.   3. Ask your teacher what type of test will be given.   4. Gather the information needed to study.   5. Use remembering strategies to remember the information.

6-2 Day 5. Highlight information to be remembered.
Day 4. Use remembering strategies.
Day 3. Rewrite information in brief form.
Day 2. Think of questions and write answers.
Day 1. Review rewritten notes and questions and answers.

6-3 D. Read test directions carefully and ask teacher to explain anything not understood.
E. Examine test to see how much there is to do.
T. Decide how much time to spend answering each item.
E. Answer easiest questions first.
R. Review answers.

6-4 Responses will vary but should conform to the formats shown for the two types.

6-5 Notes will vary.

6-6 1. d.   2. b.   3. c.   4. b.   5. b.

6-7 Notes will vary.

6-8 1. True.   2. True.   3. True.   4. False.   5. False.   6. False.   7. False.

6-9 Notes will vary.

6-10 Test One: A4;   B5;   C3;   D2;   E1.
Test Two: 1E;   2B;   3D;   4A;   5C.

6-11 Notes will vary.

6-12 1. blue.   2. 50.   3. dollar.   4. feed.   5. Pacific.   6. Thomas.   7. Bill.   8. fuels.   9. grammatically.   10. answer.

6-13 Notes will vary.

6-14 1. Explain.   2. Describe.   3. Discuss.   4. Explain.   5. Describe.   6. Discuss.

6-15 Responses may vary. Suggested responses are: 1. Compare.   2. Evaluate or criticize.   3. Trace.   4. List or summarize.

6-16 Suggested answers follow:
1. Exercise should be an important part of everyone's life. [Describe] how exercise can help you to lead a healthy and satisfying life.
2. Controversy still exists about whether the United States was right to fight a war in Vietnam. [Trace] the events that led to our involvement in the Vietnam war.
3. The Constitution of the United States is the document that established the national government of the United States. [Explain] what the Founding Fathers tried to accomplish when they wrote this important document.
4. Communism remains a major economic and political system in many parts of the world. [Compare] the communist and democratic forms of government with respect to election of leaders.
5. [Discuss] the major positions taken by George W. Bush as he campaigned to be elected in 2000.

6-17 Responses will vary but should contain the information presented in 6-2. Here is an example of an appropriate response:

A five-day test preparation plan helps you get ready for a test and get a high score on the test. You need to begin studying five days before the test. On the fifth day before a test, get all the information you need to know. On the fourth day, use remembering strategies to remember the information. On the third day, rewrite the information in the fewest words. On the day before the test, think of questions that your teachers might ask and write answers for each. On the day of the test, review one last time. The five-day test preparation strategy will make you prepared for your test and improve your grades.

6-18 1. 60 minutes. 2. First item. 3. Responses may vary. Sample responses are: Item 1, 20 minutes; Item 2, 15 minutes; Item 3, 15 minutes; Item 4, 10 minutes. 4. Responses will vary. 5. Responses will vary. 6. Revise your planned use of time.

6-19 Responses will vary.

6-20 1. Same as for 6-1. 2. Same as for 6-2. 3. Multiple-choice: Guidelines shown on 6-5; True/false: Guidelines shown on 6-7; Matching: Guidelines shown on 6-9; Completion: Guidelines shown on 6-11. 4. same as for 6-13.

Reflection Responses will vary but should reveal insights into how the student has become a better learner.

## CHAPTER SEVEN

Using Reference Sources

TITLES OF REPRODUCIBLE ACTIVITIES

USING THE REPRODUCIBLE ACTIVITIES

After you have distributed a reproducible activity, here are suggestions for its use. Define any terms and clarify any concepts students do not know. Feel free to add further information, illustrations, or examples. Wherever possible, relate the activity to actual subject-area assignments.

7-1 Learning about Types of Reference Sources

Traditional reference sources owned by libraries in print formats are among the most authoritative sources for factual information. Most have a reputation for using experts to compile and write the information provided, and their standards for quality control are usually rigorous. The most frequently used types of reference sources are dictionaries, encyclopedias, thesauruses, almanacs, atlases, and biographical sources. Activities are included in this chapter for each of these sources.

Use the graphic organizer and text to acquaint students with frequently used types of reference sources. Show examples of these types of reference sources. Have students answer the questions. Ask students to share what they wrote about their experiences using reference sources.

7-2 Learning about Electronic Reference Sources

Increasingly, many publishers of traditional print reference sources are publishing their products in electronic formats, including CD-ROM and on the Internet via the World Wide Web. In many cases, the electronic versions offer additional features, such as the ability to search by keywords using Boolean connectors; hyperlinked words, phrases, and images to click on and jump to related information; and multimedia applications such as audio, video, and animation. Some electronic versions of reference sources are text-only without any multimedia features. Usually the text of the electronic version is the same as the print version.

Using electronic reference sources requires basic computer skills, such as keyboard/mouse skills; the ability to select and use keywords and Boolean connectors; and some familiarity with tool/task bars, pop-up windows, scrolling, and navigating. Furthermore, schools must have the resources to provide access to electronic reference sources on computers for students.

Use the graphic organizer and text to acquaint students with the formats for electronic reference sources. Have students complete the activity. Ask students to share what they wrote about their experiences using electronic reference sources.

7-3 Learning about Dictionaries

Use the Venn diagram graphic organizer and text to acquaint students with abridged and unabridged dictionaries. Show students examples of each type. Have students answer the questions.

7-4 Using a Dictionary

Have students read about the different types of information found on a dictionary page. Explain any terms they do not understand. Point out that there may be variations between dictionaries but that the basic information remains the same. Then have students complete the activity.

7-5 Using Different Dictionaries

Use this activity to have students look for and use different kinds of dictionaries at home and in the library. Tell students that they may need to use more than one dictionary to find information about a word. Then have them look up the meaning of the word *joculator*. This fairly obscure word was chosen so that students will likely have to use more than one dictionary. You may provide additional words, but be sure that they are words *not* included in some dictionaries. Have students answer the questions.

7-6 Using a Thesaurus

Review the introductory text with students. Show the students any thesauruses that may be available. Have students use a thesaurus to find synonyms for the words. Point out that they must pay attention to the form of the word listed (e.g., noun, verb).

7-7 Learning about Encyclopedias

Encyclopedias make up a large part of a library's reference collection. They are known for their accuracy, expertise, and currency. Encyclopedias vary in the features they provide. There are four main types of encyclopedias: general, single volume, children and young adult, and subject encyclopedias. For each type, many different titles are available, published by different publishers. For example, some encyclopedias for children and young adults are the *World Book Encyclopedia, Compton's Interactive Encyclopedia 2000, Grolier's New Book of Knowledge,* the *Oxford Children's Encyclopedia,* and the *Children's Britannica.*

Review the introductory text with students. Have students read about the four types of encyclopedias. Then have them write what is contained in each.

7-8 Learning about Electronic Encyclopedias

Many publishers now offer their encyclopedias in both print and electronic formats. The electronic version may be on CD-ROM, as are the multimedia encyclopedias frequently sold with new computers, or it may be available on the Internet. Sometimes the electronic version of an encyclopedia is multimedia and sometimes it is text only.

Another possibility is that the electronic encyclopedia may be made available on a network. For example, in the state of Florida, the *Encyclopedia Britannica* is available in school and public libraries throughout the state.

Review the differences between print and multimedia encyclopedias. Then have students complete the activity. To answer questions 5 and 6, students will need to apply what they learned in previous activities. Have students share their responses to these two questions.

7-9 Locating Print and Electronic Encyclopedias

Have students complete the activity. Remind students to ask the librarian for assistance if they cannot find one or more of the types of encyclopedias.

7-10 Using a Print Encyclopedia

Tell students that they should always use the index of an encyclopedia because they may not find information about a topic in the volume in which they expect it to be. For example, a student looking for information about *cars* might go to the "C" volume but may not find an entry for *cars*. However, if the student looks for *cars* in the index volume, the entry for *cars* may provide a cross-reference to the "A" volume for *automobiles*, or the T volume for *transportation*.

Demonstrate how a keyword and index can be used to locate information about a topic in a print encyclopedia. Use the sample index entry to explain the types of information found in an encyclopedia index entry. Then have students look at the sample entry for "Moon" and answer the questions.

7-11 Using a Multimedia Encyclopedia

Use this activity only if the students have access to a multimedia encyclopedia.

Multimedia encyclopedias on CD-ROM are very common and may be included with the purchase of a new computer. Using a multimedia encyclopedia successfully requires basic computer skills: keyboard/mouse skills, scrolling, using navigation buttons, and some familiarity with tool/task bars and pop-up windows.

Multimedia encyclopedias use many icons to help identify the different media included in an article. The icon used may vary with the product, but the media identified are the same. For example, an icon for a map may be a globe in one product but a compass in another.

Have students read the introductory text about icons. Go over each of the examples with students. Then have them use a multimedia encyclopedia to find information about Haiti. For each icon, have them write what happened when they clicked on the icon and what they learned about Haiti.

Depending on the multimedia encyclopedia used by the students, not all icons may be found. You may substitute another country or provide more countries from which students can choose.

7-12 Using an Almanac

Review the introductory text with students. Then tell them to use the index to find facts in an almanac. Caution students that, depending on the almanac they use, the index may be in the front, middle, or back. Have students locate almanacs in the library to complete the activity. Tell them to use the current edition. You can use this activity as a group project or as a competition between individuals and/or groups. Later, have students share their experiences in using almanacs to locate facts.

7-13 Using an Atlas

As with encyclopedias, there are different types of atlases. A general world atlas contains maps showing physical and political features of countries throughout the world. Most general world atlases include sections of maps on specific topics, such as climate, population, or health. A historical atlas contains maps that portray an event or show how something developed or changed over a period of time. Historical atlases include information about topics such as changes in borders, military campaigns, exploration, or culture. A subject atlas contains maps related to a specific place or topic. Atlases are available in both print and electronic formats.

Review the introductory text with students. Emphasize that students may have to use more than one type of atlas to answer the questions. Help students locate atlases to complete the activity. You can use this activity as a group project or as a competition between individuals and/or groups. Later, have students share their experiences in using atlases to locate information.

7-14 Using an Electronic Atlas

Use this activity only if your students have access to an electronic atlas or to the World Wide Web.

Many atlases are published in both print and electronic formats. The electronic version may be on CD-ROM, as are the multimedia atlases sometimes included with new computers, or it may be available on the Internet, as is the atlas available at the National Geographic web site. Find out if your library has an electronic atlas.

Review the introductory text with students. Then have them use an electronic atlas to find information about Sudan. Have students answer the questions about the information they found. Then lead a discussion about the differences between print and multimedia atlases. Ask students to share their experiences using an electronic atlas.

7-15 Finding Biographical Information

Biographical reference sources provide information about famous people, living or dead. Some biographical sources provide information about authors only. Students can often find information about more people in these sources than in any other sources.

Biographical sources are also published in both print and electronic format. Electronic biographical sources are available on CD-ROM as well as on the World Wide Web.

Review the difference between a biography and an autobiography with students. Tell them that they may find information about a person in an encyclopedia, but that biographical sources often provide more information than encyclopedias. Also point out that biographical sources contain information about people who do not appear in encyclopedias. Then have students locate information about each person listed using biographical sources in your library.

7-16 Mastery Assessment and Reflection

Have students complete this assessment when you believe they have learned about reference sources and how and when to use them. Review the results of the assessment with the students. Provide additional instruction as necessary.

Reference sources are used to find background information on a topic, to find facts, and to get a quick answer to a question. Look at the graphic organizer for types of reference sources. Then read about it.

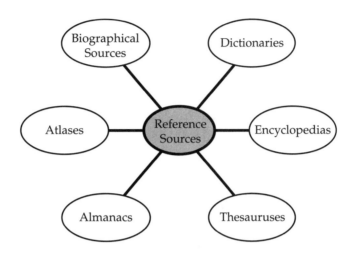

The most frequently used types of reference sources are dictionaries, encyclopedias, thesauruses, almanacs, atlases, and biographical sources. Reference sources are usually shelved in their own section of the library. Ask the librarian to help you locate reference sources.

1. What are three uses of reference sources?

_____

_____

2. What are the six most frequently used types of reference sources?

_____

_____

3. Who can help you locate reference sources?

_____

_____

4. What reference sources have you used in the past?

_____

_____

Look at the graphic organizer for **electronic reference sources**. Then read about it.

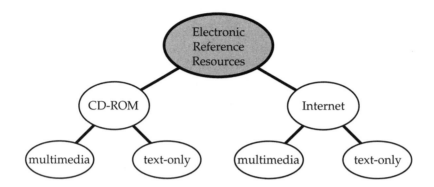

Many reference sources are available in electronic formats. The graphic organizer shows that the two most common electronic formats are CD-ROM and the Internet.

The graphic organizer also shows that the CD-ROM is available in both multimedia and text-only formats. The Internet also offers both multimedia and text-only formats.

Multimedia formats contain images, sound, video, and/or animation in addition to text. Text-only formats contain text but do not include images, sound, video, and animation.

1. In what two electronic formats are reference sources available?

   _____

   _____

2. What do multimedia reference sources contain?

   _____

   _____

3. What are text-only CD-ROM reference sources?

   _____

   _____

4. What electronic reference sources have you used in the past?

   _____

   _____

Look at the graphic organizer for dictionaries. Then read about it.

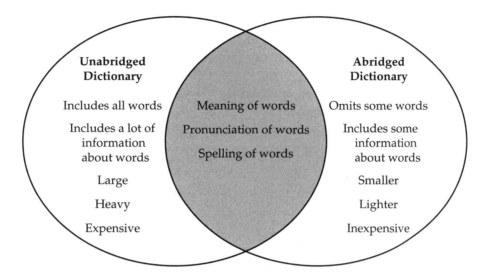

Dictionaries are reference books that provide information about the meaning, pronunciation, and spelling of words. Two important types of dictionaries you should know about are unabridged dictionaries and abridged dictionaries.

Unabridged Dictionaries   **Unabridged dictionaries** attempt to include all words currently in use in a language. Because they include all the words and a lot of information about the words, unabridged dictionaries are very large and heavy. They usually are expensive. An example of an unabridged dictionary is the *Random House Dictionary of the English Language*.

Abridged Dictionaries   **Abridged dictionaries** include only the words most frequently used in a language. Because they include fewer words and less information about the words, they are smaller, lighter, and less expensive than unabridged dictionaries. An example of an abridged dictionary is the *American Heritage Dictionary*.

1. What information do dictionaries provide?

   _____

2. What type of dictionary includes almost every word that people use today?

   _____

3. How is an abridged dictionary different from an unabridged dictionary?

   _____

4. What type of dictionary is smaller, lighter, and less expensive?

   _____

Read about the types of information you will find on a dictionary page. Refer to this information to complete the activity.

1. **Guide words:** There are two guide words at the top of every page in a dictionary. The first guide word is called the *opening guide word*. It shows the first word on the page. The second guide word is called the *closing guide word*. It shows the last word on the page.

2. **Entry words:** Entry words are the words listed and defined on the page. They are in bold type to make them easy to locate.

3. **Phonetic respellings:** Each entry word is followed by a phonetic respelling, usually in parentheses. The respelling uses symbols and letters to show you how to pronounce the word.

4. **Part of Speech:** After the respelling you usually will find an abbreviation that tells the part of speech for the entry word. The abbreviation is often in italics. Here are the abbreviations you will find for the common parts of speech:

n = noun	*v* = verb	*adj* = adjective
pron = pronoun	*adv* = adverb	*prep* = preposition

5. **Definitions:** The definitions for each entry word are included. They are numbered to show how commonly they are used. The most common definition is listed as **1.** The next most common definition follows as **2,** and so on.

6. **Variants of the Word:** The entry word may also include different forms of the word. For example, *directed, directing,* and *directs* may be included with the entry word *direct.*

7. **Origin or etymology:** Some dictionaries include information telling the language from which the word came. Sometimes this information is in brackets [ ]. In some cases, an abbreviation for the original language may be included, such as G for Greek or L for Latin.

8. **Usage:** In some cases, a sentence containing the entry word is provided to show how the word might be used.

9. **Synonym or antonym:** Sometimes a synonym and/or an antonym for the entry word is provided. The abbreviation *syn* is used for synonyms, and *ant* is used for antonyms.

10. **Illustration:** Sometimes drawings or photographs are included to illustrate the word.

11. **Short and long pronunciation keys:** The *short pronunciation key* is usually found at the bottom of the right-hand dictionary page. It contains letters, symbols, and words that will help you pronounce words correctly. If the short pronunciation key does not help you pronounce an entry word, then look at the *long pronunciation key* found at the front of your dictionary. These pronunciation keys can be used to help you understand the phonetic respellings.

Here is a sample entry from a dictionary. In each box, place the number from the previous page for its description.

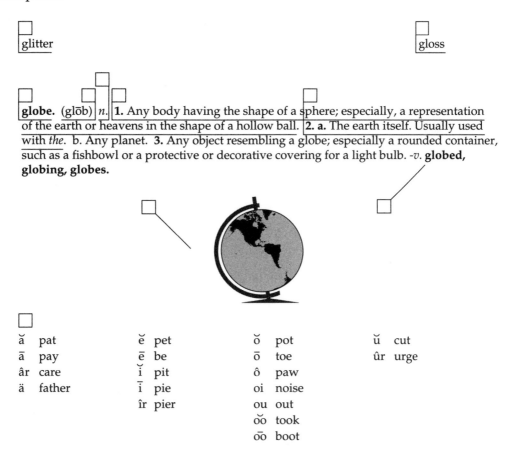

☐ glitter

☐ gloss

☐ **globe.** (glōb) *n.* **1.** Any body having the shape of a sphere; especially, a representation of the earth or heavens in the shape of a hollow ball. **2. a.** The earth itself. Usually used with *the*. b. Any planet. **3.** Any object resembling a globe; especially a rounded container, such as a fishbowl or a protective or decorative covering for a light bulb. *-v.* **globed, globing, globes.**

☐ ă pat   ĕ pet   ŏ pot   ŭ cut
ā pay   ē be   ō toe   ûr urge
âr care   ĭ pit   ô paw
ä father   ī pie   oi noise
   îr pier   ou out
   ŏŏ took
   ōō boot

Using Different Dictionaries

If you cannot find a word in one dictionary, try another. You may need to use a larger, unabridged dictionary to find your word.

Look up the following word: *joculator*

Answer the questions:

1. What is the most common definition for *joculator*?

2. What is the title of the dictionary in which you found this word?

3. Is this an abridged or unabridged dictionary?

4. In how many dictionaries did you look before you found this word?

Using a Thesaurus

A **thesaurus** is a reference source that contains synonyms for commonly used words. A **synonym** is a word having the same or nearly the same meaning as another word. Words in a thesaurus are listed in alphabetical order. Following each word is its part of speech and a list of synonyms. You use a thesaurus to select words that will help you express an idea precisely.

Use a thesaurus to find synonyms for the following words. Write down all the synonyms you find.

1. **grab**

   _____

   _____

2. **command**

   _____

   _____

3. **hurricane**

   _____

   _____

4. **struggle** (*n*)

   _____

   _____

5. **tired**

   _____

   _____

6. **mild**

   _____

   _____

7. **crowd** (*v*)

   _____

   _____

Learning about Encyclopedias

An **encyclopedia** contains articles written by experts on a variety of subjects. The articles are arranged in alphabetical order by topic. There are four types of encyclopedias with which you should be familiar:

1. **General encyclopedias** include overview articles on a wide range of topics. The articles are arranged alphabetically in a set of volumes. Illustrations are also included. The last volume in the set is the index. Information is kept up-to-date with articles published in yearbooks or supplements. An example of a general encyclopedia is the *Encyclopedia Americana*.

2. **Single-volume encyclopedias** include short articles arranged in alphabetical order. There is no index or table of contents. An example of a single-volume encyclopedia is the *Random House Concise Encyclopedia*.

3. **Encyclopedias for children and young adults** are general encyclopedias written for a specific age group. The articles include many illustrations and study aids and are easier to read than articles in other encyclopedias. An example of an encyclopedia for children and young adults is the *World Book Encyclopedia*.

4. **Subject encyclopedias** are found for many subjects, such as geography, science, and art. Some are written for adults, others for younger students. Articles in a subject encyclopedia are longer and more technical than those found in general encyclopedias. An example of a subject encyclopedia is *Dorling Kindersley's Encyclopedia of Science*.

What is contained in each of the following?

1. General encyclopedias:

   _____

   _____

2. Single-volume encyclopedias:

   _____

   _____

3. Encyclopedias for children and young adults:

   _____

   _____

4. Subject encyclopedias:

   _____

   _____

Electronic encyclopedias are used with a computer. Two formats for electronic encyclopedias are CD-ROM and the Internet.

Encyclopedias on CD-ROM may be multimedia or text-only. Multimedia encyclopedias include images, sound, video, and/or either animation as well as text. Text-only electronic encyclopedias do not include pictures or any other media.

Encyclopedias on the Internet also may be either multimedia or text-only. Multimedia encyclopedias on CD-ROM are the most popular format of electronic encyclopedia. An example of a multimedia encyclopedia on CD-ROM is *Multimedia Encyclopedia of Science & Technology*.

1. What are two formats for electronic encyclopedias?

   _____

   _____

2. What does a multimedia encyclopedia include that a text-only encyclopedia does not?

   _____

   _____

3. What is the most popular format of electronic encyclopedia?

   _____

   _____

4. Describe an experience you have had using an electronic encyclopedia.

   _____

   _____

5. What do you think are some advantages to using a multimedia encyclopedia instead of a print encyclopedia?

   _____

   _____

6. What do you think are some advantages to using a print encyclopedia instead of a multimedia encyclopedia?

   _____

   _____

Find an example of each of the following types of encyclopedias. Write its title and call number. Then ✔ **Print** or **Electronic** to show the format of the encyclopedia that you found.

General Encyclopedia

Title _____

Call number _____

Print _____ Electronic _____

Encyclopedia for Children and Young Adults

Title _____

Call number _____

Print _____ Electronic _____

Subject Encyclopedia

Title _____

Call number _____

Print _____ Electronic _____

Single-Volume Encyclopedia

Title _____

Call number _____

Print _____ Electronic _____

To look for information in an encyclopedia, begin by selecting the most important word in your topic. This word is your **keyword**. Look for your keyword in the index to the encyclopedia. The index is usually the last volume. Select another word in your topic if you cannot find your first keyword in the index.

Using the keyword *moon* from the topic "Space exploration and the moon," you might find the following index entry. Study this sample index entry and answer the questions.

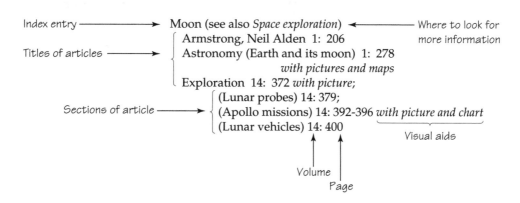

1. What is the index entry?

   _____

   _____

2. Where would you look for more information about the index entry?

   _____

   _____

3. What are the titles of the articles for the index entry?

   _____

   _____

4. In the article "Armstrong, Neil Alden 1: 206," what does "1" stand for?

   _____

5. In the article "Armstrong, Neil Alden 1: 206," what does the "206" stand for?

   _____

Using a Multimedia Encyclopedia

Icons are used to find information in a multimedia encyclopedia. An **icon** is a hyperlinked image used in a computer database. Here are some common icons you might find when using a multimedia encyclopedia. Look at each icon to learn what it stands for and what happens when you click on it.

Icon	*What it stands for:*	*What happens when you click on it:*
	Video	Videoclip appears. *Example:* Scenes of hurricanes and the destruction they cause.
	Sound	Sound occurs. *Examples:* Alligator growl; rap group performing; audio broadcast of astronaut when man first landed on the moon.
	Animation	Movement occurs. *Example:* Diagram of how a rocket works, showing various stages and narrated with an explanation of each step in the process.
	Picture	Picture appears. *Examples:* Photograph of a platypus, famous athlete, movie star.
	Map	Map appears. *Example:* Map of the Middle East with names of places hyperlinked.
	Table/chart/graph	Table, chart, or graph appears. *Example:* Chart showing endangered plants and animals, graph showing world population, table showing characteristics of the moon.

Use a multimedia encyclopedia to look up the country *Haiti*. Find each of the following icons or the icon used by that encyclopedia for that function. Click on each. Write what happened. Then write a statement that explains what you learned.

1.

What happened when I clicked on it: _____

What I learned about Haiti: _____

2.

What happened when I clicked on it: _____

What I learned about Haiti: _____

3.

What happened when I clicked on it: _____

What I learned about Haiti: _____

4.

What happened when I clicked on it: _____

What I learned about Haiti: _____

5.

What happened when I clicked on it: _____

What I learned about Haiti: _____

6.

What happened when I clicked on it: _____

What I learned about Haiti: _____

Using an Almanac

An **almanac** is a single-volume reference book containing facts on a wide range of topics. Almanacs are revised each year so that the facts they contain are current. Some frequently used almanacs are the following:

> *Time Almanac 2000*
> *New York Public Library Desk Reference*
> *World Almanac and Book of Facts*

Use the current edition of one of these almanacs or any other almanac to answer the questions that follow. You may need to look in more than one almanac. Write down the title of the almanac containing the facts needed to answer the question and the page number(s) on which the facts were found.

1. What is the name of the largest nuclear power plant in the United States?

   Answer: _____

   Title of Almanac: _____

   Page(s): _____

2. What was the population of the United States in 2000?

   Answer: _____

   Title of Almanac: _____

   Page(s): _____

3. What language is spoken by the most people in the world?

   Answer: _____

   Title of Almanac: _____

   Page(s): _____

Using an Atlas

An **atlas** is a collection of maps. There are many different types of atlases. Two common atlases are the following:

Hammond Historical Atlas of the World
Times Atlas of World History

Go to your library and find the atlases available there. Write the names of at least two here.

Use an atlas to answer the questions that follow. You may need to use more than one atlas. Write the title of the atlas containing the information needed to answer the question and the page number(s) on which the information was found.

1. What are the names of the countries that border Libya on the continent of Africa?

   Answer: _____

   Title of Atlas: _____

   Page(s): _____

2. What is the name of the mountain range in Russia that is east of Moscow?

   Answer: _____

   Title of Atlas: _____

   Page(s): _____

3. Find a map that shows the average rainfall of Puerto Rico. How many inches of rain fall in Puerto Rico in one year?

   Answer: _____

   Title of Atlas: _____

   Page(s): _____

Using an Electronic Atlas

Atlases can be found in electronic formats. They are on CD-ROM and on the Internet. Some atlases on CD-ROM or on the Internet are multimedia.

Two popular atlases on CD-ROM are the following:

Eyewitness World Atlas
Hammond Atlas of the World

National Geographic Society also has a free *Map Machine Atlas* on the World Wide Web at:

http://www.nationalgeographic.com/resources/ngo/maps/index.html

Use an electronic atlas to look up the country *Sudan*. Use the atlas to answer these questions.

1. Did you find a political map of Sudan?

   _____

2. Did you find a physical map of Sudan?

   _____

3. What other maps did you find for Sudan?

   _____

4. Can you find a map of Sudan by typing in the name of the country?

   _____

5. Can you zoom in on a region in Sudan?

   _____

6. Did you find an article about Sudan?

   _____

7. Did you find any photographs?

   _____

8. What did you like best about using the electronic atlas?

   _____

   _____

Finding Biographical Information

Biographical sources are reference books that provide information about the lives and accomplishments of famous people, living or dead. The entries vary in length from one paragraph to several pages.

Some common biographical sources are the following:

Something about the Author
Dictionary of Scientific Biography
Webster's Biographical Dictionary

Biographical sources are also available in electronic format. A useful biographical source is:

Biographies Illustrated Plus

Use this biographical source or any other biographical source in your library to find information about the famous people that follow. Next to each name, write the title of the biographical source containing information about that person. Also write the page number(s) where the information appears. If there is a volume number, write that, too.

	Title of Biographical Source	*Volume/Page(s)*
Harriet Tubman	_____	_____
Jackie Robinson	_____	_____
John Glenn	_____	_____
Louisa May Alcott	_____	_____
Cesar Chavez	_____	_____
George W. Bush	_____	_____

See what you have learned about using reference sources.

1. What are the six most frequently used types of reference sources?

   _____

2. What is the difference between multimedia and text-only reference sources?

   _____

3. What is an abridged dictionary?

   _____

4. What is a thesaurus?

   _____

5. What are four types of encyclopedias?

   _____

6. What are two formats for electronic encyclopedias?

   _____

7. What information does the index entry for an encyclopedia provide?

   _____

8. What is an icon?

   _____

9. What is an almanac?

   _____

10. What is an atlas?

    _____

11. What are biographical sources?

    _____

Reflection How has learning to use reference sources made you a better student?

_____

_____

ANSWER KEY FOR CHAPTER SEVEN

7-1 1. To find background information on a topic, to find facts, and to get a quick answer to a question.   2. Dictionaries, encyclopedias, thesauruses, almanacs, atlases, and biographical sources.   3. Librarian.   4. Responses will vary.

7-2 1. CD-ROM; Internet.   2. Images, sound, video, animation, and/or text.   3. Reference sources that contain text but do not contain images, sound, video, or animation.   4. Responses will vary.

7-3 1. Information about the meaning, pronunciation, and spelling of words.   2. Unabridged.   3. Omits words that are not frequently used; contains less information about words; is smaller, lighter, and less expensive.   4. Abridged.

7-4

1
glitter

1
gloss

4

2 3 5   5

globe. (glōb) *n.* **1.** Any body having the shape of a sphere; especially, a representation of the earth or heavens in the shape of a hollow ball. **2. a.** The earth itself. Usually used with *the.* b. Any planet. **3.** Any object resembling a globe; especially a rounded container, such as a fishbowl or a protective or decorative covering for a light bulb. *-v.* **globed, globing, globes.**

10

6

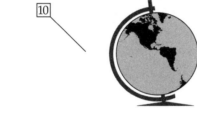

11

ă	pat	ě	pet	ŏ	pot	ŭ	cut
ā	pay	ē	be	ō	toe	ûr	urge
âr	care	ĭ	pit	ô	paw		
ä	father	ī	pie	oi	noise		
		îr	pier	ou	out		
				ŏŏ	took		
				ōō	boot		

7-5 1. The first definition of *joculator* is: "a professional jester, a person who amuses others."   2. Responses will vary.   3. Responses will vary.   4. Responses will vary.

7-6 Responses will vary.

7-7 1. Overview articles on a wide range of topics.   2. Short articles arranged in alphabetical order.   3. Articles that include many illustrations and study aids and that are easier to read than articles in other encyclopedias.   4. Long and technical articles.

7-8 1. CD-ROM; Internet.   2. Images, sound, video, and/or animation.   3. Multimedia encyclopedias on CD-ROM.   4. Responses will vary.   5. Responses will vary but may include: "Can combine keywords to search for topics"; "Can see images and videos and hear sounds, more fun."   6. Responses will vary but may include: "More people can use it at once"; "Don't need a computer"; "Don't need to know how to use a computer."

7-9 Responses will vary.

7-10 1. Moon.   2. Space exploration.   3. Armstrong, Neil Alden; Astronomy (Earth and its moon); Exploration.   4. Volume.   5. Page.

7-11 1. Movement occurs; information about Haiti will vary.   2. Sound occurs; information about Haiti will vary.   3. Map appears; information about Haiti will vary. 4. Table/chart/graph appears; information about Haiti will vary.   5. Picture appears; information about Haiti will vary.   6. Videoclip appears; information about Haiti will vary.

7-12 1. Houston Power and Light.   2. Approximately 280 million.   3. Mandarin. (Titles and pages will vary with almanac used.)

7-13 1. Algeria; Tunisia; Egypt; Sudan; Chad; Niger.   2. Ural Mountains.   3. Approximately 59 inches.

7-14 Responses will vary depending on the electronic atlas used.

7-15 Responses will vary.

7-16 1. Dictionaries, encyclopedias, thesauruses, almanacs, atlases, and biographical sources. 2. Multimedia sources contain images, sound, video, animation, and/or text; text-only sources contain only the text.   3. A dictionary that includes only the words most frequently used in a language.   4. A reference source that contains synonyms for commonly used words.   5. General, single-volume, encyclopedias for children and young adults, and subject encyclopedias.   6. CD-ROM and Internet.   7. Titles of articles, sections of articles, volume(s), page(s), visual aids, and where to look for more information.   8. Hyperlinked image used in a computer database.   9. A single-volume reference book containing facts on a wide range of topics.   10. A collection of maps. 11. Reference books that provide information about the lives and accomplishments of famous people, living or dead.

Reflection Responses will vary but should reveal insights into how the student has become a better learner.

## CHAPTER EIGHT

Writing a Research Paper

TITLES OF REPRODUCIBLE ACTIVITIES

USING THE REPRODUCIBLE ACTIVITIES

After you have distributed a reproducible activity, here are suggestions for its use. Define any terms and clarify any concepts students do not know. Feel free to add further information, illustrations, or examples. Wherever possible, relate the activity to actual subject-area assignments.

8-1 A Strategy for Writing a Research Paper

Use the activity to activate students' prior knowledge. Then have students share what they do for each step. Have students correct and add to what they wrote. Conclude by telling students that they will be learning about these steps as they complete the activities in this chapter.

8-2 Learning about Choosing a Topic

Use the introductory text to help students learn about topics that are too broad, too narrow, or just right. Have students explain why each topic is too broad, too narrow, or just right.

The first topic is too broad because there is a vast amount of information available about space flight. It would take students a very long time to locate all the sources, read them, and then write a paper within the number of pages assigned.

The second topic is too narrow because it focuses on one very specific aspect of space flight. Students will find it difficult to find enough information to write a paper.

The third topic is just right because there is enough information available to write a paper, but not so much that the students will be overwhelmed by the amount of information.

8-3 Practice Choosing a Topic

Review with students what they have learned in 8-2. Then have students use this activity to identify topics as too broad, too narrow, or just right.

8-4 Knowing If You Have Chosen a Good Topic

When the students have completed the activity, call on students to explain why they chose particular topics.

8-5 Locating Sources of Information

Students will have to go to the library to complete this activity. Encourage them to look for electronic sources of information such as on CD-ROM. Eliminate the web page as a source if students do not have access to the World Wide Web in your school.

8-6 Preparing Bibliography Cards
8-7 Preparing Bibliography Cards for Electronic Sources

Explain the importance of using bibliography cards to document sources of information used when writing research papers. Tell students they must prepare a separate bibliography card for each source of information, whether print or electronic. Use the sample cards to explain how bibliography cards are prepared for each type of source of information. Point out that for a given information source, the citation may not include all the parts called for on a bibliography card. For example, the author might not be identified.

Point out that information for bibliography cards for electronic sources comes from the computer record. The headings on a computer record will not necessarily match the headings required for a bibliography card. Students will have to match the information on a computer record with the information needed for a bibliography card.

Have students prepare bibliography cards for the six types of sources of information found in 8-5.

8-8 Preparing Note Cards

Explain to students why they need to prepare note cards. Have students refer to the sample bibliography card and the note cards that go with it. Tell students that they must follow the five steps as they prepare note cards for their papers.

As students follow these five steps, point out that articles such as *the*, *a*, and *an* should not be considered the first word when alphabetizing. Emphasize the need for legible writing. Remind students to use abbreviations, acronyms, and other brief forms to reduce the amount of text they write.

Have students use what they learned to prepare note cards for their papers.

8-9 Writing the Outline

Explain to students why they need to prepare an outline. Have students refer to the sample outline. Identify the main topic, subtopics, details, and subdetails. Tell students that they must follow the seven steps as they prepare an outline for their papers.

Have students use what they learned to prepare outlines for their papers.

8-10 Writing the Draft

Tell students to write a draft of their research papers. Use the text and sample pages to explain the parts of a research paper that must be included in a draft. Point out that not all sections of a research paper are included in a draft. The title page (8-12), table of contents (8-13), and bibliography (8-14) will be added when preparing the final paper.

Have students follow the five steps to write the drafts of their research papers. Tell them they must double-space their drafts to leave room for revisions.

8-11 Revising the Draft

Show students how to use the Revising Checklist to revise their drafts.

8-12 Preparing the Title Page

Use the introductory text and sample title page to explain what a title page contains and how to prepare it. Then have students prepare title pages for their papers.

8-13 Preparing the Table of Contents

Use the introductory text and sample table of contents to explain what a table of contents contains and how to prepare it. Have students prepare tables of contents for their papers.

8-14 Preparing the Bibliography

Use the introductory text and sample bibliography to explain what a bibliography is and how to prepare it. Have students prepare bibliographies for their papers.

8-15 Final Checklist

Discuss with students how to use the Final Checklist to be sure their papers are ready to hand in. Then have students complete the Final Checklist. Help students to make any revisions necessary until they can answer yes to all the questions.

8-16 Mastery Assessment and Reflection

Have students complete this assessment when you feel they have learned the ten steps in writing a research paper. Review the results of the assessment with the students. Provide additional instruction as necessary.

Think about what you know about writing a research paper. Then read the following steps in a strategy for writing a research paper. As you read each step, write what you know about the step.

Step 1: Choose a topic.

_____

Step 2: Locate sources of information.

_____

Step 3: Prepare bibliography cards.

_____

Step 4: Prepare note cards.

_____

Step 5: Write the outline.

_____

Step 6: Write the paper.

_____

Step 7: Prepare a bibliography.

_____

Step 8: Prepare a title page.

_____

Step 9: Prepare a table of contents.

_____

Step 10: Check your paper before handing it in to your teacher.

_____

The first step in writing a research paper is to **choose a topic.** If the topic you choose is **too broad,** there will be too much information to find, read, and understand in the time you have available to complete the paper. If the topic you choose is **too narrow,** you will not find enough information to write about. You must choose a topic that is **just right.** This means that you can find enough sources to complete your paper in the time you have available. It also means that you can write your paper within the number of pages assigned by your teacher.

1. The following topic is too broad. Write a statement telling why.
   Topic: **The history of space flight.**

   _____

   _____

   _____

   _____

   _____

2. The following topic is too narrow. Write a statement telling why.
   Topic: **Reentry to the earth's atmosphere during space flight.**

   _____

   _____

   _____

   _____

   _____

3. The following topic is just right. Write a statement telling why.
   Topic: **Space flight to the moon.**

   _____

   _____

   _____

   _____

   _____

Practice Choosing a Topic

In each box there are three related topics. One is too broad, one is too narrow, and one is just right. Write *too broad, too narrow,* or *just right* below each topic.

---

1. The role of nurses at the Battle of Gettysburg

_____

The Civil War

_____

Battle of Gettysburg

_____

---

2. Mammals in the sea

_____

Orcas in Alaska

_____

Migrating whales

_____

---

3. Buddhism

_____

Religions of the world

_____

Buddhist monks in training

_____

Here are some important questions you should answer about any topic you choose. These questions will help you know if the topic you have chosen is a good one.

Write three topics about which you might write a research paper.

Topic 1

_____

_____

Topic 2

_____

_____

Topic 3

_____

_____

For each topic, answer questions 1–4 on a separate piece of paper, then answer 5 and 6.

1. *Is the topic too broad, too narrow, or just right?*
   Remember, if the topic is too broad or too narrow, you will find it difficult to complete the paper as required by your teacher.

2. *Does your library have enough information available on the topic?*
   Check in the library to see if there are enough sources on the topic. Make sure you have at least as many sources as required by your teacher.

3. *Are you interested in the topic?*
   Be sure to select a topic about which you are interested. It takes a lot of time to do the research and writing. If you are not interested in the topic, you will probably not do a very good job of writing the paper.

4. *Will your teacher approve the topic?*
   Show your written topic to your teacher and ask for approval. Do not begin to work on a topic unless your teacher has approved it.

5. Choose one of the topics approved by your teacher for your research paper. Write it here.

6. Why did you choose this topic?

In the space below, write the topic you selected in 8-4.

Find information on your topic in each of the following sources. For each source, write down its title and call number. For the first five sources, also ✔ whether it is in Print or Electronic format. Include at least one source that is in electronic format.

1. **Encyclopedia:**

   Title: _____

   Call Number: _____   Print _____   Electronic _____

2. **Other Reference Book:**

   Title: _____

   Call Number: _____   Print _____   Electronic _____

3. **Book:**

   Title: _____

   Call Number: _____   Print _____   Electronic _____

4. **Magazine:**

   Title: _____

   Call Number: _____   Print _____   Electronic _____

5. **Newspaper:**

   Title: _____

   Call Number: _____   Print _____   Electronic _____

6. **Audiovisual:**

   Title: _____

   Call Number: _____

7. **World Wide Web**

   Title of web page: _____

   URL (address): _____

Bibliography cards are used to keep a record of the sources from which you obtained information for your paper. Look at how information is written on each bibliography card. Use these sample bibliography cards as models to prepare bibliography cards for sources you located in 8-5. You will learn about preparing bibliography cards for electronic sources in 8-7.

Encyclopedia
"Space Exploration." Encyclopedia
Americana. 2000 ed.

Other Reference Book
Curtis, Anthony R. Space Almanac:
Facts, Figures, Names, Dates, Places,
Lists, Charts, Tables, Maps Covering
Space from Earth to the Edge of the
Universe. Woodsboro, MD: Arcsoft,
1989.

Book
Von Bencke, Matthew J. The Politics of
Space: A History of U.S.–Soviet/
Russian Competition & Cooperation.
Boulder, CO: Westview Press, 1997.

Magazine Article
Steacy, Anne. "A Step in Time."
Macleans 24 Jul. 1989: 47.

Newspaper Article
"Moon Landing Was Worth the Cost:
(Results of CBS News Public Opinion
Polls on Moon Landing in 1969)" New
York Times 24 Jul. 1994, nat'l ed.: E5.

Audiovisual
Moon Shot Videorecording: The Inside
Story of the Apollo Project. Prod. and
Dir. Kirt Woltinger. Videocassette. TBS
Productions Inc. Varied Directions
International, Dist. Atlanta: Turner
Home Entertainment, 1994.

Here is a sample bibliography card for a magazine article on CD-ROM. You may also find articles from newspapers and encyclopedias on CD-ROM. They may be full text or citation only. Headings are provided for each part of the citation shown on the sample card.

Electronic Database

Author(s):	Keefe, Ann.
Title of Article:	"July 20, 1969: The Greatest Adventure."
Title of Publication:	*Cobblestone: The History Magazine for Young People.*
Date of Article/Page(s):	Jan. 1995: 36–41.
Title of Database:	*ProQuest Periodical Abstracts-Library.*
Publication Medium:	CD-ROM.
Name of Vendor:	UMI Company.
Date of CD-ROM:	1996.

Here is a sample bibliography card for a web page found on the World Wide Web. Headings are provided for each part of the citation shown on the sample card.

World Wide Web Source

Author(s):	Dunbar, Brian.
Title:	*Apollo 11.*
Date of Information:	29 Mar. 1996.
Site:	National Aeronautics and Space Administration.
Address (URL):	http://www.nasa.gov/hqpao/apollo_11.html
Online Service:	World Wide Web, Netscape.
Date Accessed:	15 Mar. 1997.

Use these sample bibliography cards as models for preparing your own bibliography cards. Prepare bibliography cards for any types of sources you located in 8-5.

Look at the sample bibliography card and the note cards that go with it. Note cards are used to write notes or quotes from the source listed on the bibliography card. You must prepare one or more note cards for each bibliography card.

Sample Bibliography Card   *Sample Note Cards*

⑦

Magazine Article

Steacy, Anne. "A Step in Time." *Macleans* 24 Jul. 1989: 47.

---

⑦-1

President Nixon said "Because of what you have done, the heavens have become part of man's world." p47

Pope Paul VI cautioned not to put human achievement above God's.

---

⑦-2

It took $26 billion and 8 yrs after JFK set goal.

1969–72—9 astro reached the moon

VP Agnew predicted man on Mars

Follow these steps as you prepare note cards for your paper.

Step 1: Arrange your bibliography cards in alphabetical order by the first word on the card.

Step 2: Number your bibliography cards starting with 1 for the first card. Write the number in the upper right-hand corner as in the sample bibliography card.

Step 3: Number your note cards using two numbers separated by a dash as in the sample note cards. Write the number in the upper right-hand corner. In the sample note card numbered 7-1, 7 shows that the notes are for the source listed on bibliography card 7, and -1 shows that this is the first card used to record notes from this source. A second note card would be numbered 7-2, and so on.

Step 4: Circle the numbers on the note cards to keep them separate from other numbers you might write when taking notes.

Step 5: Write notes on the note cards. Use your own words whenever possible. Place quotation marks around all quotes. Write the page number on which each quote appears.

Look at the sample outline for a research paper. It shows how to organize information from your note cards into main topics, subtopics, details, and subdetails.

Space Flight to the Moon

I. Manned space programs
   A. U.S. programs
      1. Mercury, Gemini, Apollo
         a. Apollo 11
   B. Soviet programs
      1. Vostok, Voskhod, Soyuz
   C. Accidents and other setbacks
      1. 1967 accidents
         a. Apollo
         b. Soyuz
      2. Apollo 13
II. The U.S.–Soviet race for the moon
   A. The cost of competition
      1. How much did it all cost?
      2. Was it worth it?
   B. Comparing technology
III. Looking back to the first step
   A. Anniversary celebrations
   B. Lunar projects since Apollo 17

Follow these steps as you prepare an outline for your paper.

Step 1: Write the title of the research paper.

Step 2: Organize the notes from your note cards into main topics.

Step 3: Write the Roman numeral I and after it the first main topic. Write the Roman numeral II for the second main topic, and so on.

Step 4: Write the subtopics that go with the first main topic. Use capital letters before each subtopic.

Step 5: Write the details that go with each of these subtopics. Use Arabic numerals before each detail.

Step 6: Write the subdetails that go with each of these details. Use small letters before each subdetail.

Step 7: Repeat Steps 4, 5, and 6 for each main topic.

Writing the Draft

A **draft** is a paper you write that must be revised before it becomes your final paper. Read about the parts of a research paper that you must include in your draft. Look at the sample pages that show where the parts are located in the research paper. Follow these steps as you write a draft of your research paper.

Step 1: Write the **title** at the top of the page. The title is a short statement that tells the subject of your paper.

Step 2: Write an **introduction** that introduces the topic and tells the reader what your paper will be about. The introduction is a paragraph or two at the beginning of a paper.

Step 3: Write the **body** of your paper. It begins after the introduction and ends before the conclusion. The body includes headings and the text that goes with them. The body is the longest part of the paper, usually several pages.

Step 4: Insert any pictures, drawings, charts, and other **visual aids** that will help the reader understand what you are writing about in your paper.

Step 5: Write a **conclusion**. The conclusion tells the reader what you have learned about the topic or summarizes your point of view.

Space Flight to the Moon   1   **Step 1**
This paper is about the history of space   **Step 2**
flight to the moon. It includes information
about…xxxxxxxxxxxxxxxxxxxxxxxxxxx
xxxxxxxxxxxxxxxxxxxxxxxxxxxxxxxx
xxxxxxxxxxxxxxxxxxxxxxxxxxxxxxxx
xxxxxxxxx
Manned Space Programs   **Step 3**

The United States and the Soviet Union
had the two major programs for putting
man on the moon…xxxxxxxxxxxxxxxxxx

2

Two major accidents occurred in 1967, one
in the U.S. and one in the Soviet Union.
Each caused setbacks to the space
programs.xxxxxxxxxxxxxxxxxxxxxxxxxxx
xxxxxxxxxxxxxxxxxxxxxxxxxxxxxxxx
xxxxxxxxxxxxxxxxxxxxxxxxxxxxxxxx

The U.S.-Soviet Race for the Moon

Both Russia and the United States wanted
to put man on the moon first. The
competition was fierce, costing both
nations millions of dollars.xxxxxxxxxxx
xxx
xxx
xxx

3

Many Americans questioned whether or
not the space program was worth the $26
billion spent but…xxxxxxxxxxxxxxxxxxx
xxxxxxxxxxxxxxxxxxxxxxxxxxxxxxxx   **Step 4**
xxxxxxxxxxxxxxxxxxxxxxxxxxxxxxxx

xxxxxx	xxxxxxxxx	xxxxxxx
xxxxxx	xxxxxxxx	
xxxxxx	xxxxxxxx	xxxxxxx

Table showing cost of Apollo Program
xxxxxxxxxxxxxxxxxxxxxxxxxxxxxxxxxx
xxxxxxxxxxx …xxxxxxxxxxxxxxxxxxxx
xxxxxxxxxxxxxxxxxxxxxxxxxxxxxxxx
xxxx
xxxx

4

Looking Back—NASA Projects since 1969

There have been many celebrations since
1969. There have also been several lunar
projects. One interesting project was the
building of the space stationxxxxxxxxxxxx
xxxxxxxxxxxxxxxxxxxxxxxxxxxxxxxxxx

Conclusion   **Step 5**

In conclusion, the history of space flight to
the moon is ….xxxxxxxxxxxxxxxxxxxxxxxx

Use the **Revising Checklist** to learn what changes you may need to make in the draft of your paper. Place a ✔ next to each question for which you can answer YES. Revise your draft until you can check YES for all questions.

Revising Checklist

_____ **1.** Does the introduction clearly introduce the topic?

_____ **2.** Did I include headings to help the reader understand the topic?

_____ **3.** Does the body of the paper contain all facts needed?

_____ **4.** Does each paragraph contain a main idea?

_____ **5.** Does every paragraph and sentence add something to the paper?

_____ **6.** Did I choose the best words to explain ideas?

_____ **7.** Does my conclusion follow from the facts?

_____ **8.** Did I spell all words correctly?

_____ **9.** Did I capitalize words as needed?

_____ **10.** Is there subject-verb agreement in all cases?

_____ **11.** Are tenses consistent?

_____ **12.** Are all sentences complete?

_____ **13.** Did I use quotation marks to identify all quotations?

_____ **14.** Did I number the pages correctly?

_____ **15.** Do I have a one-inch margin at the top, bottom, and both sides?

_____ **16.** Have I reread the paper several times to find ways to improve it?

The **title page** is the first page of the research paper. It must include the title of the paper, the name of the writer, the name of the teacher, and the date the paper is due.

Look at the sample title page. Follow these steps to prepare a title page for your paper.

1. Center and type the title. Use all caps or bold to highlight it.

2. Three lines below the title, center and type the word *by*. Three lines below the word *by*, center and type your name.

3. Two lines below your name, center and type the date that the paper is due.

4. Four lines from the bottom margin, center and type *For:* followed by your teacher's name.

Space Flight to the Moon

by

Rosa Garcia

May 7, 2001

For: Ms. Blair

The **table of contents** is the second page of the research paper. It must include the introduction, all headings, conclusion, and bibliography.

Look at the sample table of contents. Follow these steps to prepare a table of contents for your paper.

1. Type "Table of Contents" at the top of a page with the first letter of the word "Table" and the first letter of the word "Contents" capitalized.

2. Type each entry and the page number on which it begins. Capitalize the major words in each entry.

3. Use dashes or dots to connect the entry to its page number.

Table of Contents

Page

Introduction 1

Manned Space Programs 1

U.S. Programs 2

Soviet Programs 3

Accidents 4

The U.S.–Soviet Race for the Moon 5

The Cost of Space Flight to the Moon 6

Technology 6

NASA Projects Since 1969 7

Conclusion 7

Bibliography 8

The **bibliography** provides a list of all the sources you used to gather information for the paper. It is included at the end of your paper.

Look at the sample bibliography below. Follow these steps to prepare a bibliography for your paper.

1. Type the word *Bibliography* at the top of a page in the center.

2. Put your bibliography cards in alphabetical order by the first word on each card.

3. Type the information as it appears on each bibliography card. Indent the second and following lines as shown on the sample bibliography.

Bibliography

Curtis, Anthony R. Space Almanac: Facts, Figures, Names, Dates, Places, Lists, Charts, Tables, Maps Covering Space from Earth to the Edge of the Universe. Woodsboro, MD: Arcsoft, 1989.

Dunbar, Brian. Apollo 11. 29 Mar. 1996. National Aeronautics and Space Administration. http://www.nasa.gov/hqpao/apollo_11.html World Wide Web, Netscape. 15 Mar. 1997.

Keefe, Ann. "July 20, 1969: The Greatest Adventure." Cobblestone: The History Magazine for Young People Jan. 1995: 36–41. ProQuest Periodical Abstracts-Library. CD-ROM. UMI Company, 1996.

"Moon Landing Was Worth the Cost: (Results of CBS News Public Opinion Polls on Moon Landing in 1969)" New York Times 24 Jul. 1994, nat'l ed.: E5.

Moon Shot Videorecording: The Inside Story of the Apollo Project. Prod. and Dir. Kirt Woltinger. Videocassette. TBS Productions Inc. Varied Directions International, Dist. Atlanta: Turner Home Entertainment, 1994.

"Space Exploration." Encyclopedia Americana. 2000 ed.

Steacy, Anne. "A Step in Time." Macleans 24 Jul. 1989: 47.

Von Bencke, Matthew J. The Politics of Space: A History of U.S.–Soviet/Russian Competition & Cooperation. Boulder, CO: Westview Press, 1997.

When you have finished writing your research paper, look it over to complete the **Final Checklist**. Place a ✔ next to each question for which you can answer YES. If you have a ✔ next to each question, your paper is ready to be handed in to your teacher. If not, revise your paper until you have a ✔ next to each question. Then your paper is ready to be handed in.

Final Checklist

_____ **1.** Do I have a title page?

_____ **2.** Do I have a table of contents?

_____ **3.** Are the pages numbered correctly?

_____ **4.** Do I have a bibliography?

_____ **5.** Do I have a second copy for myself?

_____ **6.** Do I have a folder in which to place the original copy to hand in to my teacher?

See what you have learned about writing a research paper.

1. How many important steps must you follow to write a research paper?

    _____

2. What problem will you have if you choose a topic that is too broad? Too narrow?

    _____

3. List seven types of sources that you may use to locate information for your topic.

    _____

4. What is the purpose of bibliography cards?

    _____

5. On a note card, what does **6-2** mean?

    _____

6. Label each part of the following outline:

    I. _____

        A. _____

            1. _____

                a. _____

7. What is the first page of the research paper called? The second page?

    _____

8. What is a bibliography?

    _____

9. What is the purpose of the final checklist?

    _____

Reflection How has learning a strategy for writing a research paper made you a better student?

_____

_____

ANSWER KEY FOR CHAPTER EIGHT

8-1 Notes will vary.

8-2 Responses will vary but should include these ideas: 1. Too much information to find, read, and understand. 2. Not enough information to write about. 3. The right number of sources to write a paper within time and length constraints.

8-3 1. Too narrow, too broad, just right. 2. Too broad, too narrow, just right. 3. Just right, too broad, too narrow.

8-4 Responses will vary.

8-5 Responses will vary.

8-6 Bibliography cards will vary.

8-7 Bibliography cards will vary.

8-8 Note cards will vary.

8-9 Outlines will vary.

8-10 Drafts will vary.

8-11 Responses will vary.

8-12 Title pages will vary.

8-13 Tables of contents will vary.

8-14 Bibliographies will vary.

8-15 Responses will vary.

8-16 1. Ten. 2. Will not be able to complete the paper in the number of pages assigned; will not be able to find enough information. 3. Encyclopedia; other reference book; book; magazine; newspaper; audiovisual; web page from the World Wide Web.
4. To keep a record of the sources of information used for the paper.
5. Bibliography card 6, note card 2.
6. I. Main Topic
    A. Subtopic
       1. Detail
          a. Subdetail
7. Title Page; Table of Contents. 8. A list of all the sources used to gather information for a paper. 9. To be sure a paper is ready to be handed in.

Reflection Responses will vary but should reveal insights into how the student has become a better learner.

## CHAPTER NINE

Pronouncing Big Words

TITLES OF REPRODUCIBLE ACTIVITIES

USING THE REPRODUCIBLE ACTIVITIES

After you have distributed a reproducible activity, here are suggestions for its use. Define any terms and clarify any concepts students do not know. Feel free to add further information, illustrations, or examples. Wherever possible, relate the activity to actual subject-area assignments.

9-1 The P2SWA Word Attack Strategy for Pronouncing Big Words

Tell students they will be learning a strategy for pronouncing big words they do not recognize when reading. Have students write a paragraph explaining what they do to pronounce the big word *subscription*. Conclude by having students write a statement telling what they think each word in P2SWA tells them to do when pronouncing a big word.

9-2 Learning about P2SWA

Use this activity to explain each step in the P2SWA strategy. Have students apply the steps to the word *repairing*. Have students identify a reference that will help them identify how to pronounce words.

9-3 Understanding How P2SWA Is Used

This activity uses modeling to show how a student uses P2SWA to pronounce a big word. Call upon individual students to give their own modeling statements for the steps in P2SWA for multisyllable words you select.

9-4 Putting It All Together

Have students complete this page on their own to demonstrate that they understand the steps in the P2SWA strategy. Have students share how they think the strategy makes them a better reader.

9-5 Forming Words with Prefixes

Use this activity to introduce students to some common prefixes. Feel free to have students add other prefixes to the page. Have students read aloud the words they formed to be certain they consist of a prefix and stem.

9-6 Forming Words with Suffixes

Use this activity to introduce students to some common suffixes. Feel free to have students add other suffixes to the page. Have students read aloud the words they formed to be certain they consist of a stem and suffix.

9-7 Forming Words with Prefixes and Suffixes

Use this activity to give students an opportunity to separate prefixes and suffixes from stems. This is similar to what they do when confronted with an unrecognized big word prior to attempting to pronounce the word. Have students demonstrate their mastery by writing words consisting of prefix and stem, stem and suffix, and prefix, stem, and suffix.

9-8 Dividing Multisyllable Stems: VC/CV

Use the activity to show students how to divide multisyllable stems into separate syllables when the letters are arranged into the VC/CV (vowel-consonant/consonant-vowel) pattern. Conclude by having the students write the rule they learned for dividing multisyllable stems into syllables.

9-9 Dividing Multisyllable Stems: V/CV

Use the activity to show students one way to divide stems that follow the VCV pattern. Since the first syllable ends in a vowel, the vowel is pronounced with the long sound. Conclude by having students write the rule.

9-10 Dividing Multisyllable Stems: VC/V

Use this activity to show students a second way to divide stems that follow the VCV pattern. Since the first syllable ends in a consonant, the vowel is pronounced with the short sound. Conclude by having students write the rule.

Tell students that they often have to use both pronunciation rules (V/CV and VC/V) to discover which one will be useful for pronouncing unrecognized words. Their ear will tell them which pronunciation is correct. Students will need to do this when completing activities in 9-13.

9-11 Applying P2SWA

Have students read the sentence and apply P2SWA to the underlined word. Have students write statements explaining what they are to do when using the steps in the strategy.

9-12 Practice Using P2SWA
9-13 More Practice Using P2SWA

Use these activities to provide additional practice using P2SWA to pronounce multisyllable words.

9-14 Mastery Assessment and Reflection

Have students complete this assessment when you believe they have learned to use P2SWA strategy presented in this chapter. Review the results of the assessment with students. Provide additional instruction as needed.

The P2SWA Word Attack Strategy for Pronouncing Big Words

A big word has two or more syllables. *Subscription* is a big word. Write a paragraph that tells what you would do to pronounce this big word.

_____

_____

_____

_____

_____

_____

_____

_____

_____

_____

_____

You will learn how to use the P2SWA strategy for pronouncing big words as you read. Each of the following words is an important part of the strategy. Write what you think each word tells you to do when pronouncing a big word.

P2SWA Strategy

Prefix _____

Suffix _____

Stem _____

Word Building _____

Ask _____

Big words have two or more syllables. This is how to use P2SWA to pronounce big words.

Prefix   **Look for a prefix.** Many big words begin with a prefix. A prefix is a syllable that is added to the beginning of a word.

The prefix is circled in *prepayment*. Circle the prefix in *repairing*.

(pre)payment   1. repairing

Suffix   **Look for a suffix.** Many big words end with a suffix. A suffix is a syllable that is added to the end of a word. The suffix is circled in *prepayment*. Circle the suffix in *repairing*.

prepay(ment)   2. repairing

Stem   **Look for a stem.** Once the prefix and/or suffix are removed from a word, what remains is the stem. The stem is circled in *prepayment*. Circle the stem in *repairing*.

pre(pay)ment   3. repairing

Word Building   **Build and pronounce the word.** Blend the prefix, stem, and suffix together to pronounce the word. Write the word once you have pronounced it.

4. re + pair + ing = _____

Ask   **Ask for help.** If you still cannot pronounce the word, ask your teacher or another student to help you. If necessary, use a reference book that will help you pronounce words you do not recognize. Write the name of a reference book you might use here.

5. _____

Here is how Angela used P2SWA to pronounce the underlined word in the following sentence.

It is <u>rewarding</u> to get a good grade on a test.

Prefix   Angela did not recognize the underlined word. She looked at the word to see if it began with a prefix she recognized. She recognized *re* as a *prefix*.

Suffix   Angela knew she should look for a suffix next. She recognized *ing* as a *suffix*.

Stem   Angela looked to see what was left without the prefix and the suffix. She was left with *ward* and recognized it as the *stem*.

Word Building   Angela said each part of the word alone: *re*, then *ward*, and then *ing*. Then she blended the parts together to pronounce the whole word.

re+ward+ing = rewarding

Ask   Because Angela was able to pronounce the word *rewarding*, she did not have to ask for help. If she had not been able to pronounce the word, she could have asked her teacher or another student for help. Or she could have used the phonetic respelling found in a dictionary for the entry word *rewarding*.

Complete the following to show that you know how to use P2SWA to pronounce the underlined word:

Iced tea is a great <u>refreshment</u> on a hot day.

Prefix   Write the prefix.   1. _____

Suffix   Write the suffix.   2. _____

Stem   Write the stem.   3. _____

Word Building   Write what you should do to pronounce the word.

4. _____

_____

_____

Ask   Write what you should do if you cannot pronounce the word.

5. _____

_____

6. How can P2SWA make you a better reader?

_____

_____

_____

_____

_____

_____

_____

_____

_____

Forming Words with Prefixes

After each **prefix** is a **stem**. Add the prefix to the stem and write the **whole word**. Then write **another word** that begins with the same prefix. The first one is done for you.

Prefix	Stem	Whole Word	Another Word
ab	sent	absent	abnormal
de	fine	_____	_____
pro	noun	_____	_____
be	come	_____	_____
un	done	_____	_____
in	ability	_____	_____
ad	verb	_____	_____
sub	side	_____	_____
ex	act	_____	_____
com	press	_____	_____
re	forest	_____	_____
en	close	_____	_____
dis	grace	_____	_____
pre	heat	_____	_____
anti	social	_____	_____
in	active	_____	_____
bi	cycle	_____	_____
ir	regular	_____	_____
tri	angle	_____	_____
kilo	gram	_____	_____
il	legal	_____	_____
im	balance	_____	_____

Forming Words with Suffixes

Before each **suffix** is a **stem**. Add the suffix to the stem and write the **whole word**. Then write **another word** that ends with the same suffix. The first one is done for you.

Stem	*Suffix*	*Whole Word*	*Another Word*
hope	ful	hopeful	graceful
mail	able	_____	_____
love	ly	_____	_____
walk	ing	_____	_____
high	er	_____	_____
talk	ed	_____	_____
move	ment	_____	_____
act	ive	_____	_____
skill	ed	_____	_____
kind	ness	_____	_____
east	ern	_____	_____

Forming Words with Prefixes and Suffixes

Look at each word. Some words have a prefix, some have a suffix, and some have a prefix and a suffix. For each word:

> Write the prefix, if there is one.
> Write the suffix, if there is one.
> Write the stem.
> Write and pronounce the word.

The first one is done for you.

Word	Prefix	Suffix	Stem	Word
camping		ing	camp	camping
reboarding	_____	_____	_____	_____
mainly	_____	_____	_____	_____
enrichment	_____	_____	_____	_____
unsinkable	_____	_____	_____	_____
installment	_____	_____	_____	_____
remove	_____	_____	_____	_____
entrenchment	_____	_____	_____	_____
unknowing	_____	_____	_____	_____

Write your own word that has a prefix and stem: _____

Stem and suffix: _____

Prefix, stem, and suffix: _____

When a stem has more than one syllable, you must divide it into separate syllables to pronounce it.

Look at these stems: *attic, button*. You can see that each has a vowel followed by a consonant, and then a consonant followed by a vowel. This is known as the VCCV pattern. The rule for dividing a stem that has this pattern is to divide the stem between the two consonants. Here is how it is done:

VC / CV   VC / CV

at / tic   but / ton

Here are some stems that follow the VC/CV pattern. Draw a slash to divide each stem into two syllables.

1. p e r s o n

2. p e n c i l

3. c i r c u s

4. s u m m e r

5. c a n c e l

6. c a t t l e

7. n a p k i n

8. c e n t e r

9. b a r t e r

10. s i l v e r

11. c a r g o

12. g r a m m a r

13. Write the rule you learned for dividing stems into syllables.

_____

_____

_____

_____

_____

Look at these stems: *hotel, station*.

Each has two syllables that follow the VCV pattern. For each of these stems, the first vowel is pronounced with the long sound. The rule for dividing a stem in this case is to divide the stem after the first vowel. Here is how to do this.

V / C V	V / C V
ho / tel	sta / tion

Here are some stems that follow the V/CV pattern. For each stem the first vowel has the long sound. Draw a slash to divide each stem into two syllables.

1. d i r e c t   **2.** f a m o u s

3. p u p i l   **4.** sp i d e r

5. l o c a t e   **6.** f i n a l

7. b l a t a n t   **8.** p i r a t e

9. l e g a l   **10.** n a s a l

11. Write the rule you learned for dividing stems into syllables.

_____

_____

_____

_____

_____

Look at these stems: *river, habit*.

Like the stems in 9–9, each has a vowel followed by a consonant followed by a vowel (VCV). Here the first vowel is pronounced with the short sound. The rule for dividing a stem in this case is to divide the stem between the consonant and second vowel. Here is how to do this.

V C / V   V C / V

r i v / e r   h a b / i t

Here are some stems that follow the VC/V pattern. For each stem, the first vowel has the short sound. Draw a slash to divide each stem into two syllables.

1. d a m a g e   2. r i g i d

3. t i m i d   4. n o v e l

5. d o z e n   6. c o m i c

7. i m a g e   8. s e v e n

9. p e t a l   10. e p i c

11. Write the rule you learned for dividing stems into syllables.

_____

_____

_____

_____

_____

Use P2SWA to attack and pronounce the underlined word. Answer the questions to explain what you did.

He was <u>abnormally</u> upset about losing the game.

1. What did you do for the Prefix step?

_____

_____

_____

2. What did you do for the Suffix step?

_____

_____

_____

3. What did you do for the Stem step?

_____

_____

_____

4. What did you do for the Word Building step?

_____

_____

_____

5. What did you do for the Ask step?

_____

_____

_____

Practice Using P2SWA

Use P2SWA to attack and pronounce the underlined words. Write what you did for each step.

The new mattress was very <u>uncomfortable</u>.

P _____

_____

S _____

_____

S _____

_____

W _____

_____

A _____

_____

The vet held the puppy very <u>tenderly</u>.

P _____

_____

S _____

_____

S _____

_____

W _____

_____

A _____

_____

Use P2SWA to attack and pronounce the underlined words. For each word explain how you used the strategy.

The <u>unopened</u> package arrived a week late.

_____

_____

_____

_____

_____

_____

He took the <u>indirect</u> route home from the park.

_____

_____

_____

_____

_____

_____

He <u>timidly</u> asked her for a date.

_____

_____

_____

_____

_____

_____

1. For each letter of P2SWA, write the word that the letter helps you remember.

   P = _____

   S = _____

   S = _____

   W = _____

   A = _____

2. Explain how P2SWA is used to pronounce a big word. Be sure to tell what you should do for each step.

   _____

   _____

   _____

   _____

   _____

   _____

   _____

Reflection How has learning a strategy for pronouncing big words made you a better student?

_____

_____

_____

_____

ANSWER KEY FOR CHAPTER NINE

9-1 Responses will vary.

9-2 1. (re)pairing. 2. repair(ing.) 3. re(pair)ing. 4. repairing. 5. Any reference book that can be used to learn the pronunciation of words, such as a dictionary.

9-3 No student response required.

9-4 1. re. 2. ment. 3. fresh. 4. Identify prefix, suffix, and stem. Blend together to pronounce word. 5. Ask for help or use a reference book. 6. Responses will vary.

9-5 Students complete the activity in the same way as the example.

9-6 Students complete the activity in the same way as the example.

9-7 Students complete the activity at the top of the page in the same way as the example. Words students write at the bottom of the page will vary.

9-8 1. per/son. 2. pen/cil. 3. cir/cus. 4. sum/mer. 5. can/cel. 6. cat/tle. 7. nap/kin. 8. cen/ter. 9. bar/ter. 10. sil/ver. 11. car/go. 12. gram/mar. 13. When stems follow the VCCV pattern, they are divided between the two consonants (VC/CV).

9-9 1. di/rect. 2. fa/mous. 3. pu/pil. 4. spi/der. 5. lo/cate. 6. fi/nal. 7. bla/tant. 8. pi/rate. 9. le/gal. 10. na/sal. 11. When stems follow the VCV pattern and the first vowel is pronounced with the long sound, divide the stem after the first vowel (V/CV).

9-10 1. dam/age. 2. rig/id. 3. tim/id. 4. nov/el. 5. doz/en. 6. com/ic. 7. im/age. 8. sev/en. 9. pet/al. 10. ep/ic. 11. When stems follow the VCV pattern and the first vowel is pronounced with the short sound, divide the stem between the consonant and second vowel (VC/V).

9-11 Student responses will vary but reflect what was learned about the P2SWA strategy.

9-12 Student responses will vary but reflect what was learned about the P2SWA strategy.

9-13 Student responses will vary but reflect what was learned about the P2SWA strategy.

9-14 1. P=Prefix, S=Suffix, S=Stem, W=Word Building, A=Ask.
2. Student responses should reflect the steps of P2SWA.

Reflection Responses will vary but should reveal insights into how the student has become a better learner.

## CHAPTER TEN

Finding Main Ideas

TITLES OF REPRODUCIBLE ACTIVITIES

USING THE REPRODUCIBLE ACTIVITIES

After you have distributed a reproducible activity, here are suggestions for its use. Define any terms and clarify any concepts students do not know. Feel free to add further information, illustrations, or examples. Wherever possible, relate the activity to actual subject-area assignments.

10-1 Learning about the READ Main Idea Strategy

Begin by having students activate their prior knowledge and write a statement that explains how they read for main ideas. Then have students take notes as you explain the READ strategy. Conclude by having students write a statement that tells which of the READ steps they included in their written statement.

10-2 Applying READ

Use 10-2 to have students apply READ to a paragraph to find and write down the main idea.

10-3 Practice Using READ

Use 10-3 to provide students with more practice in finding and writing down a main idea.

10-4 Finding the Topic Sentence
10-5 Practice Finding the Topic Sentence

Use 10-4 to review the concept of topic sentence. Have students read the paragraph and apply READ to identify and write down the topic sentence. Use 10-5 to provide more practice. 10-5 also introduces the idea that topic sentences can be found in different parts of a paragraph.

10-6 Writing Topic Sentences
10-7 Writing More Topic Sentences

Have students use READ to find and write down the topic sentence for each of three paragraphs. Then have students identify whether the three topic sentences were at the beginning, middle, or end of each paragraph.

10-8 Identifying a Passage Title

Tell students that a passage consists of two or more paragraphs on a topic. Have students write down the topic sentence for each of the three paragraphs in the passage about Yellowstone Park. Then have them choose the best title from three possible titles.

10-9 Writing a Passage Title

Have students read the three-paragraph selection about a treasure hunter. Have them use READ to find and underline the topic sentence for each paragraph. Then have students use the topic sentences to write a title. Remind students that their title should reflect the ideas of the topic sentences. Finally, have students share their titles.

10-10 Mastery Assessment and Reflection

Have students complete this assignment when you believe they have learned to use the READ strategy presented in this chapter. Review the results of the assessment with students. Provide additional instruction as needed.

Learning about the READ
Main Idea Strategy

Write a paragraph that explains what you do when reading to find the main idea of a paragraph.

_____

_____

_____

_____

Learn how the **READ strategy** is used to find main ideas. As your teacher explains each step, add any notes that will help you remember what to do.

Read the paragraph to get an idea of what it is about.

Look for words that are repeated throughout the paragraph.

Evaluate each sentence to determine the important words.

In each sentence, underline the important words that tell what the sentence is about.

Analyze the important words to learn what they have in common.

Look at the words you underlined. Write a statement that tells what they have in common.

Decide upon the main idea of the paragraph.

Look for a sentence that tells what the words you underlined have in common.
If you find such a sentence, it is the topic sentence, and you should consider it the main idea.
If you do not find such a topic sentence, use the statement you wrote for the Analyze step as the main idea.

Which of these steps did you include in the paragraph you wrote?

_____

_____

_____

Follow the steps in READ to complete this activity.

Read this paragraph to get an idea of what it is about. Look for the important words that are repeated.

Many stories are told about sharks. Some stories say that all sharks will attack people. Some stories say that sharks can smell blood from a mile away. Other stories tell us that sharks have no enemies in the deep. While these tales are not really true, many people believe them.

    1. What is the paragraph about?

_____

_____

Evaluate each sentence and underline the important words.

    2. Write the words you underlined in each sentence.

        First sentence: _____

        Second sentence: _____

        Third sentence _____

        Fourth sentence: _____

        Fifth sentence: _____

Analyze the words you underlined to determine what they have in common.

    3. Write a statement that tells what the words you selected have in common.

_____

_____

Decide upon the main idea. Is there a sentence that tells what the words you underlined have in common? If yes, it is the topic sentence, and consider it the main idea. If no, the statement you wrote for the Analyze step is the main idea.

    4. Write the main idea.

_____

_____

Read this paragraph to get an idea of what it is about.

> Not all sharks are dangerous to people. Only about 25 kinds are dangerous to people. Some of the sharks that are really dangerous to people are the great white, tiger, bull, and the hammerhead. The great white shark is the most dangerous of all.

1. What is the paragraph about?

   _____

   _____

   _____

Evaluate each sentence to determine the important words.

2. Write the words you underlined in each sentence.

   First sentence: _____

   Second sentence: _____

   Third sentence   _____

   Fourth sentence: _____

Analyze the words you underlined to determine what they have in common.

3. Write a statement that tells what the words you chose have in common.

   _____

   _____

   _____

Decide upon the main idea:

4. Write the topic sentence or the main idea.

   _____

   _____

   _____

Sometimes a single sentence in a paragraph tells the main idea. This is called the **topic sentence**.

Read this paragraph to get an idea of what it is about.

> Many of our English words have been borrowed from the languages of other countries. The word *idea* comes from the Greek word *idein,* which means "to see." It might be said that to have an idea is "to see" something new. The word *tea* comes from the Chinese word *t'e,* which sounds very much like our word. *Kayak,* a small, one-person boat, comes from the Eskimo word for a small, skin-covered boat.

1. What is the paragraph about?

_____

_____

_____

Evaluate each sentence to determine the important words.

2. Write the important words.

_____

_____

_____

Analyze to determine what the important words have in common.

3. Write a statement that tells what is in common.

_____

_____

_____

Decide upon the main idea.

4. Write the topic sentence.

_____

_____

_____

196

A topic sentence can be any sentence in a paragraph. It may be found at the beginning, middle, or end of a paragraph.

Read this paragraph to get an idea of what it is about.

In order for you to speak, air must be pushed out from your lungs. Then it passes through your throat and the voice box and past your vocal cords. If these two bands of tissue are stretched tightly, the air causes them to vibrate and make a sound. Finally, you use your lips, tongue, and teeth to shape the sounds into words. Speaking, then, involves the lungs, throat, vocal cords, voice box, and mouth.

1. What is the paragraph about?

_____

_____

_____

Evaluate each sentence to determine the important words.

2. Write the important words.

_____

_____

Analyze to determine what the important words have in common.

3. Write a statement that tells what is in common.

_____

_____

Decide upon the main idea.

4. Write the topic sentence.

_____

_____

5. Was the topic sentence at the beginning, middle, or end of the paragraph?

_____

Use READ to find and write the topic sentence for each of the following paragraphs.

About 4,000 years ago the Egyptians used pictures for numbers. A single mark meant 1, an arch showed 10, a chain showed 100, and a flower was 1,000. Many years later, the Romans developed another way of counting. They still used a mark, *I*, for 1, but they used *V* for 5, *X* for 10, *L* for 50, and *C* for 100. The numbers we use today come from the Arabs. Many ways of counting have been used by people throughout the ages.

1. _____

_____

_____

Certain plants trap insects and other small animals for food. The Venus flytrap, for one, has leaves that work like a steel trap. Another plant of this kind is the bladderwort. It catches small water animals in the tiny traps on its leaves. Pitcher plants have pitcher-shaped leaves that hold rainwater in which insects drown.

2. _____

_____

_____

A homing pigeon is a kind of pigeon that can be trained to find its way home from a far-off place. No one knows exactly how a homing pigeon knows what direction to take or where to fly to reach home. Because it is able to do this, this pigeon has been used to carry messages in a holder on its back or leg. The homing pigeon can fly between fifty and sixty miles an hour. Some have been known to fly more than a thousand miles in two days.

3. _____

_____

_____

4. Circle the places where you found the topic sentences in these paragraphs.

Beginning   Middle   End

Read each paragraph to find and write the topic sentence. Tell where you found it in the paragraph.

When you ask the age of a small child, he or she will most likely answer by raising the correct number of fingers. When you are asked your height or weight, you answer in numbers. Numbers are a very important part of our lives. Calendars and clocks tell the date and time in numbers. Many of our favorite games use numbers also.

1. Topic sentence:

_____

Location:

_____

The ancient Romans held a festival called Lupercalia on February 15. Some people think that this was the beginning of our Valentine's Day. But no one is sure. In fact, there are at least three stories to explain how Valentine's Day started. Some people think that the holiday began because the birds in England chose their mates on February 14. Others connect the holiday with two saints, both named Valentine, who lived long ago.

2. Topic sentence:

_____

Location:

_____

Deserts are hot, dry, and sandy. They do not get enough rain for growing crops. But people have brought water to the desert and have made it good farmland in many places. They have built dams on rivers to hold back the water. Canals have been dug to carry the water through the desert. And wells have been dug to give more water.

3. Topic sentence:

_____

Location:

_____

A passage is made up of two or more paragraphs on a topic. The title of a passage tells what it is about. Read the passage and follow the directions to identify a title for the passage.

Read the story below. Then follow the directions.

Yellowstone Park is the oldest and largest of the parks owned by the United States government. In 1872, it was named the country's first national park. It is made up of desert, forest, meadows, lakes, rivers, and canyons. It has more than 300 miles of roads and a thousand miles of trails for horseback riding and walking. Yellowstone has more than two million acres of land. Some of this land has been seen only by birds and other animals.

Yellowstone Park's Old Faithful is the best-known geyser in the world. It sends a tower of boiling water into the air about every sixty-five minutes. First a little water and steam come forth from the cone and then drop back. Soon more water shoots up—a little higher, then higher, until it reaches over 150 feet in the air. This beautiful show lasts about four minutes.

As the country's largest wildlife preserve, Yellowstone is home for two hundred kinds of birds and forty other kinds of animals. Bears, elk, and buffalo roam freely. Fish swim in its lakes and rivers. The park protects all animals; no hunting is allowed.

Write the topic sentence for each paragraph.

1. _____

_____

_____

2. _____

_____

_____

3. _____

_____

_____

Read the topic sentences you wrote to decide what the passage is mainly about. Then underline the best title for the passage:

4. National Parks   Yellowstone Park   Wildlife of Yellowstone Park

Read the passage. Find and underline the topic sentence in each paragraph. Think about what the topic sentences have in common. Then write a title at the top of the passage.

1. A simple walk once led to a treasure hunt. Several years ago, a man was walking along the water's edge near Vero Beach, Florida. High winds had changed the sand path where he often walked. Suddenly he noticed something too bright to be a shell shining through the sand. He had found a Spanish gold coin called a piece of eight! He believed that the coin was part of a huge treasure that came from Spanish ships that had sunk 250 years earlier.

2. This find changed the man's life, turning him into a treasure hunter. Armed with a shovel, he returned to the beach and found more old coins and other clues that led him to think that a wreck had taken place nearby. He studied old maps and charts to learn the routes the Spanish ships took. He read the stories of the handful of people who had lived through the wreck. He hired a pilot to fly a small airplane over the area to look for signs of a sunken ship. Finally, he got a boat and a crew of divers.

3. He and the other divers searched the ocean floor, where they discovered a wealth of valuable and interesting things. They turned up gold and silver bars and coins, beautiful gold chains and rings, a diamond ring, silverware, silver cups, and copper pots. They found rich silks and lovely china from the Orient. Jars once filled with oil, water, wine, and other supplies were also dug out of the ship's remains. The divers even came upon a ship's bell and sailors' tools—not that different from those used today.

4. Write a title for this passage.

_____

_____

_____

Read this passage from a tourist guidebook. Then follow the directions.

The Branton Home is the oldest building standing at the harbor of Middletown. It has been a well-known sight on Second Street for over 200 years. Repairs have been made many times, but the outside face of the building has changed very little.

Cyrus Branton, a well-to-do merchant, had the beautiful home built in 1760. It was a gift to his new wife, Abigail. A porch was built on an upper story of the building's east side. This allowed family members and servants to watch the harbor for ships that were coming in.

Today the Branton Home is owned by the City Department of History. It is open to the public Monday through Saturday. Tours are offered daily. To find out more about the Branton Home, phone the Department of History at 555-9792.

1. Write the topic sentence for each paragraph:

Paragraph 1:

_____

_____

Paragraph 2:

_____

_____

Paragraph 3:

_____

_____

2. Write a title for the passage.

_____

Reflection How has learning to use READ made you a better student?

_____

_____

_____

ANSWER KEY FOR CHAPTER TEN

10-1 Statements will vary.

10-2 1. Sharks.   2. Words underlined will vary.   3. Stories about sharks.
4. Many stories are told about sharks.

10-3 1. Kinds of sharks.   2. Words underlined will vary.   3. Sharks that are dangerous to people.   4. Not all sharks are dangerous to people.

10-4 1. Where English words come from.   2. Words students write will vary.
3. English words from other languages.   4. The first sentence.

10-5 1. What speaking involves.   2. Words students write will vary.   3. How speech is produced.   4. The last sentence.   5. End.

10-6 1. Last sentence.   2. First sentence.   3. First sentence.   4. Beginning and end.

10-7 1. Third sentence.   2. Fourth sentence.   3. Third sentence.   4. Middle.

10-8 1. First sentence.   2. First sentence.   3. First sentence.   4. Yellowstone Park.

10-9 1. First sentence.   2. First sentence.   3. First sentence.   4. Should be something like "A Search for Sunken Treasure."

10-10 1. First sentence in each of the three paragraphs.   2. A good title would be something like "The Historic Branton Home."

Reflection Responses will vary but should reveal insights into how the student has become a better learner.

## CHAPTER ELEVEN

Learning Word Meaning

TITLES OF REPRODUCIBLE ACTIVITIES

USING THE REPRODUCIBLE ACTIVITIES

After you have distributed a reproducible activity, here are suggestions for its use. Define any terms and clarify any concepts students do not know. Feel free to add further information, illustrations, or examples. Wherever possible, relate the activity to actual subject-area assignments.

11-1 Introducing the ACED Strategy for Learning the Meaning of a Word

Discuss the importance of learning the meaning of words for improving reading comprehension. Use this activity to get students to reflect upon what they do to learn the meaning of a word and to speculate on what they will learn from the key words associated with the ACED strategy.

11-2 Learning about ACED

Use this activity to demonstrate how the ACED strategy is used to learn the meaning of the target word *vote*. Have students underline the key words associated with each of the letters in the ACED acronym. Finally, have students write down the key words they underlined.

11-3 Making Associations

Have students write associations for the two target words: *ocean* and *emigrate*. Encourage students to write as many associations as possible.

11-4 Practice Collecting Information
11-5 More Practice Collecting Information

In 11-4 have students use reference books and ask you and other students for additional information about *ocean*. Encourage students to write more than five new things they learned that go with *ocean*. Conclude by having students add the information to the *ocean* Vocabulary Circle on 11-3. Repeat for 11-5 with *emigrate*.

11-6 Practice Evaluating and Integrating Associations and Information
11-7 More Practice Evaluating and Integrating Associations and Information

In 11-6 have students write three new sentences that use *ocean*. Then have students write a paragraph in which *ocean* is used three or more times. Repeat for 11-7 with *emigrate*.

11-8 Defining a Word

Have students use what they wrote on the Vocabulary Circles as well as their sentences and paragraphs to write definitions for *ocean* and *emigrate*. Conclude by having students write a statement that explains how ACED is different from what they described they did to learn the meaning of a word in 11-1.

11-9 Using ACED to Learn the Meaning of a Social Studies Word
11-10 Using ACED to Learn the Meaning of a Science Word

Have students use these two activities to practice using the ACED strategy to learn the meaning of a social studies word (11-9) and a science word (11-10).

11-11 Mastery Assessment and Reflection

Have students complete this assessment when you believe they have learned to use the ACED strategy presented in this chapter. Review the results of the assessment with students. Provide additional instruction as needed.

Introducing the ACED Strategy for Learning the Meaning of a Word

One way to be a better reader is to increase your vocabulary. The more words whose meaning you know, the better you will understand what you read.

1. Write a paragraph that tells what you do to learn the meaning of a word.

_____

_____

_____

_____

_____

_____

_____

_____

ACED is a strategy for learning the meaning of a word. Each letter stands for a step in the strategy. Read and think about each step. Then write a sentence that tells what you think each step is telling you to do.

2. <u>**A**</u> stands for **Associate**

_____

_____

<u>**C**</u> stands for **Collect**

_____

_____

<u>**E**</u> stands for **Evaluate and Integrate**

_____

_____

<u>**D**</u> stands for **Define**

_____

_____

Read to discover how to use **ACED** to learn the meaning of a word. As you read, underline the words in each step that will help you remember what to do.

Associate To learn the meaning of a word, start by writing the word in the middle of a circle. Then write whatever you know about the word on lines coming out from the circle. What you write on the lines is the information you can ASSOCIATE with the word. Look at the example using the word *vote*.

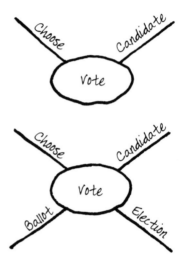

Collect Look in a dictionary, thesaurus, or encyclopedia to COLLECT information about the word. COLLECT more information about the word from your teacher and other students. Add the information to the circle. Look at the example to see how this is done.

Evaluate and Integrate Now you must evaluate and integrate your associations and the information you collected. Do this by writing two or more sentences using the word. Look at the sentences that have been written for the word *vote*.

My father cast his vote in the election.

Choose the candidate you like with your vote.

To choose by ballot or by raising hand.

Define Write a definition for the word. Keep a record of the word by writing the word and its definition in a Personal Dictionary. Use the word as often as possible when speaking and writing. This will help you remember the word and its meaning.

After each word, write the words you underlined as you read about ACED.

1. Associate: _____

2. Collect: _____

3. Evaluate and Integrate: _____

4. Define: _____

Look at the Vocabulary Circle for *ocean*. This is a familiar word about which you probably know a lot. See how many **ASSOCIATIONS** you can make for this word. Write each association on a separate line. If necessary, add more lines.

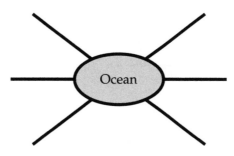

Now look at the Vocabulary Circle for *emigrate*. This may be an unfamiliar word about which you know very little. See how many **ASSOCIATIONS** you can make for this word.

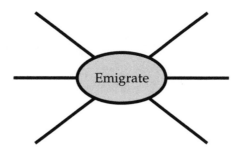

Look in a dictionary, thesaurus, or encyclopedia to **COLLECT** more information about the word *ocean*. As necessary, ask your teacher or other students about the word. Write at least five new things you learned that go with the word *ocean*.

1. _____

2. _____

3. _____

4. _____

5. _____

6. _____

7. _____

8. _____

9. _____

10. _____

Add the information to the *ocean* Vocabulary Circle on 11-3.

Look in a dictionary, thesaurus, or encyclopedia to **COLLECT** more information about the word *emigrate*. As necessary, ask your teacher or other students about the word. Then write at least five new things you learned about the word *emigrate*.

1. _____

2. _____

3. _____

4. _____

5. _____

6. _____

7. _____

8. _____

9. _____

10. _____

Add the information to the *emigrate* Vocabulary Circle on 11-3.

Look at the *ocean* Vocabulary Circle you completed for 11-3. The Vocabulary Circle contains your associations and the additional information you collected. **EVALUATE** and **INTEGRATE** what you now know about the word *ocean*. Write three sentences using the word *ocean*.

1. _____

_____

_____

2. _____

_____

_____

3. _____

_____

_____

4. Write a paragraph in which the word *ocean* is used at least three times.

_____

_____

_____

_____

_____

_____

_____

_____

_____

_____

Look at the *emigrate* Vocabulary Circle you completed for 11-3. The Vocabulary Circle contains your associations and the additional information you collected. **EVALUATE** and **INTEGRATE** what you now know about the word *emigrate*. Write three sentences using the word *emigrate*.

1. _____

_____

_____

2. _____

_____

_____

3. _____

_____

_____

4. Write a paragraph in which the word *emigrate* is used at least three times.

_____

_____

_____

_____

_____

_____

_____

_____

_____

_____

_____

1. Look at the *ocean* Vocabulary Circle you completed on 11-3. Read the sentences and paragraph you wrote on 11-6. Write a definition for the word *ocean* here.

   ocean _____

   _____

   _____

2. Look at the *emigrate* Vocabulary Circle you completed on 11-3. Read the sentences and paragraph you wrote on 11-7. Write a definition for the word *emigrate* here.

   emigrate _____

   _____

   _____

3. Look at the paragraph you wrote on 11-1 in which you described what you do to learn the meaning of a word. How is ACED different from what you wrote on 11-1?

   _____

   _____

   _____

   _____

   _____

   _____

   _____

   _____

   _____

   _____

   _____

Using ACED to Learn the Meaning of a Social Studies Word

Write a social studies word whose meaning you want to learn. Then follow the steps in the ACED strategy to learn the meaning of the word.

Social Studies word:

   1. Associate

   2. Collect

   3. Evaluate and Integrate

     Sentence 1: _____

     _____

     Sentence 2: _____

     _____

     Sentence 3: _____

     _____

     Paragraph: _____

     _____

     _____

     _____

     _____

   4. Define _____

     _____

Write a science word whose meaning you want to learn. Then follow the steps in the ACED strategy to learn the meaning of the word.

Science word:

   1. Associate

   2. Collect

   3. Evaluate and Integrate

     Sentence 1: _____

     _____

     Sentence 2: _____

     _____

     Sentence 3: _____

     _____

     Paragraph: _____

     _____

     _____

     _____

     _____

   4. Define _____

     _____

For each letter of ACED, write the word that the letter helps you remember.

A = _____

C = _____

E = _____

D = _____

Explain how ACED is used to learn the meaning of a word. Be sure to write what you should do for each step.

_____

_____

_____

_____

_____

_____

_____

_____

_____

_____

_____

Reflection How has the ACED strategy made you a better student?

_____

_____

_____

11-1 to **11-10.** Responses will vary.

11-11 A = Associate

C = Collect

E = Evaluate and Integrate

D = Define

Student explanations should reflect the ACED steps.

Reflection   Responses will vary but should reveal insights into how the student has become a better learner.

CHAPTER TWELVE

Spelling New Words

TITLES OF REPRODUCIBLE ACTIVITIES

USING THE REPRODUCIBLE ACTIVITIES

After you have distributed a reproducible activity, here are suggestions for its use. Define any terms and clarify any concepts students do not know. Feel free to add further information, illustrations, or examples. Wherever possible, relate the activity to actual subject-area assignments.

12-1 Learning about the SCVCR Spelling Strategy

Use the first activity on the page to have students explain what they do to learn how to spell a word. Let students share their strategies. Then explain the SCVCR spelling strategy. Conclude by having students write a statement that tells which of the SCVCR steps they included in their written statement.

12-2 My Personal Spelling List

Introduce "My Personal Spelling List." Tell students that they will be using this list throughout the activities. Review the directions for using the list.

12-3 Seeing How SCVCR Is Used

Have students read to learn how Andy used SCVCR to learn to spell the word *combine*. Elaborate on the steps as necessary.

12-4 Review Routines

Use 12-4 to introduce three review routines for learning the spelling of words. The routines are applied during the Review step of SCVCR. The first routine focuses on **Say and Spell**, the second on **Arrange and Spell**, and the third on **Complete and Spell**. Elaborate on these routines and then allow students to add and share routines of their own. Students will be using these routines throughout the remaining activities.

12-5 Using SCVCR to Learn to Spell Science Words
12-6 Using SCVCR to Learn to Spell Social Studies Words
12-7 Using SCVCR to Learn to Spell Language Arts Words
12-8 Using SCVCR to Learn to Spell Math Words
12-9 Using SCVCR to Learn to Spell Music and Art Words
12-10 Using SCVCR to Learn to Spell Recreation Words

Each of these activities is designed to have students use SCVCR to spell words from different content areas. Have students use the prompts to remember what to do for each step. Space is provided for students to write whatever is necessary as they go through the steps. Have students use their own paper as needed. Add words to the list or delete words as appropriate.

12-11 Using SCVCR to Learn to Spell Words You Choose
12-12 Using SCVCR to Learn to Spell Words Your Teacher Chooses

Use 12-10 to have students use SCVCR to master the spelling of words chosen by the student. Use 12-11 with words you choose. Write these words on each student's activity sheet.

12-13 Mastery Assessment and Reflection

Have students complete this assessment when you believe they have learned to use the SCVCR spelling strategy presented in this chapter. Review the results of the assessment with students. Provide additional instruction as needed.

Think about what you do to learn how to spell a word. Then write a paragraph that explains what you do.

_____

_____

_____

_____

_____

_____

_____

Read to understand how the SCVCR spelling strategy is used to learn to spell words. As your teacher explains each step, underline the words that will help you remember what to do.

Say the word. If you are not sure how to pronounce the word, ask someone or look in a dictionary to learn its pronunciation. Copy the word. Be sure you spell the word correctly.

Count the number of syllables you hear as you say the word again. Say each syllable by itself. Spell each syllable.

Visualize the spelling of the word with your eyes closed. Open your eyes and without looking at the word, write the word.

Compare your spelling of the word with the correctly spelled word. If you spelled the word correctly, write it on "My Personal Spelling List." If not, look at the correct spelling of the word and repeat the Visualize and Compare steps. Do this until you correctly spell the word. Write the word on "My Personal Spelling List."

Review the word after writing it on "My Personal Spelling List."

Which of these steps did you include in the paragraph you wrote?

_____

_____

_____

_____

My Personal Spelling List

To Use This List   Decide if your new spelling word is EASY or HARD for you to spell. If you have to repeat the Visualize and Compare steps of the SCVCR spelling strategy when learning to spell the word, it is probably a HARD word for you to spell. Write the word in the EASY or HARD column. Review the spelling of these words. Words in the HARD column should be reviewed more frequently than those in the EASY column.

EASY WORDS	*HARD WORDS*	*EASY WORDS*	*HARD WORDS*

Here is how Andy used SCVCR to learn to spell the word *combine* in the following sentence:

When you *combine* the colors blue and yellow, you get green.

Say   Andy knew how to pronounce this word. He said the word aloud and then copied it.   *combine*

Count   Andy said the word again and counted the number of syllables he heard. He wrote the number here: *2*

             Andy then said and spelled each syllable. *com bine*

Visualize   Andy then closed his eyes and visualized how the word *combine* is spelled. He then opened his eyes and wrote the word without looking at it. Here is what he wrote. *cambin*

Compare   Andy compared his spelling with the correct spelling of the word. He saw that he had not spelled *combine* correctly. He repeated the Visualize step. Here is what he wrote. *combine*

             Andy repeated the Compare step and saw that he had spelled *combine* correctly. He then went to the Review step.

Review   Andy added the new spelling word to his "My Personal Spelling List." Because he had to repeat the Visualize and Compare steps, he wrote *combine* under the heading HARD WORDS.

EASY WORDS	*HARD WORDS*
	combine

Here are three **Review Routines** to use to remember how to spell words. Use these routines with words you write on "My Personal Spelling List."

Use these routines more often for Hard Words.

SAY AND SPELL

Review Routine:
1. **Say** the word aloud.
2. Say aloud and spell each syllable.
3. **Spell** the word aloud.
4. Write the word three times.

ARRANGE AND SPELL

Materials Needed: One-inch squares of paper, each with one of the letters of the word written on it. Arrange in mixed-up order.
Review Routine:
1. **Arrange** the squares to spell the word.
2. Say the word aloud.
3. **Spell** the word aloud.
4. Write the word three times.

COMPLETE AND SPELL

Materials Needed: A sheet of paper on which the word has been written five times, each time with one or more letters missing.
Review Routine:
1. **Complete** the five words by writing the missing letter(s).
2. Write the word.
3. **Spell** the word aloud.
4. Write the word three times.

Write your own Review Routine.

_____

_____

_____

_____

_____

Using SCVCR to Learn to Spell Science Words

Look at the science words. Place a ✔ in front of two words you want to learn to spell.

> planet   chemistry   molecule
>
> protein   hibernate   nucleus
>
> Fahrenheit   pollination   species

Write one word at the top of each column. Follow the steps in SCVCR to learn to spell each word. Use the prompts to help you remember what to do. In each box write what is needed or place a ✔ to show that you have completed the task.

	Word: _____	Word: _____
Say		
Say word		
Copy word		
See if correct		
Count		
# syllables		
Spell each syllable		
Visualize		
See word in mind		
Write word from memory		
Compare		
See if correct		
Repeat steps if incorrect		
Add to "My Personal Spelling List"		
Review		
Say and Spell		
Arrange and Spell		
Complete and Spell		

Using SCVCR to Learn to Spell
Social Studies Words

Look at the social studies words. Place a ✔ in front of two words you want to learn to spell.

country	population	foreign
census	suburb	poverty
election	Constitution	minority

Write one word at the top of each column. Follow the steps in SCVCR to learn to spell each word. Use the prompts to help you remember what to do. In each box write what is needed or place a ✔ to show that you have completed the task.

Word: _____   Word: _____

Say

Say word		
Copy word		
See if correct		

Count

# syllables		
Spell each syllable		

Visualize

See word in mind		
Write word from memory		

Compare

See if correct		
Repeat steps if incorrect		
Add to "My Personal Spelling List"		

Review

Say and Spell		
Arrange and Spell		
Complete and Spell		

Using SCVCR to Learn to Spell Language Arts Words

Look at the language arts words. Place a ✔ in front of two words you want to learn to spell.

> literature   pronoun   author
> research   character   glossary
> index   grammar   punctuation

Write one word at the top of each column. Follow the steps in SCVCR to learn to spell each word. Use the prompts to help you remember what to do. In each box write what is needed or place a ✔ to show that you have completed the task.

	Word: _____	Word: _____
Say		
Say word		
Copy word		
See if correct		
Count		
# syllables		
Spell each syllable		
Visualize		
See word in mind		
Write word from memory		
Compare		
See if correct		
Repeat steps if incorrect		
Add to "My Personal Spelling List"		
Review		
Say and Spell		
Arrange and Spell		
Complete and Spell		

Using SCVCR to Learn to Spell Math Words

Look at the math words. Place a ✔ in front of two words you want to learn to spell.

estimate	average	circle
decimal	equation	operation
polygon	rectangle	percent

Write one word at the top of each column. Follow the steps in SCVCR to learn to spell each word. Use the prompts to help you remember what to do. In each box write what is needed or place a ✔ to show that you have completed the task.

	Word: _____	Word: _____
Say		
Say word		
Copy word		
See if correct		
Count		
# syllables		
Spell each syllable		
Visualize		
See word in mind		
Write word from memory		
Compare		
See if correct		
Repeat steps if incorrect		
Add to "My Personal Spelling List"		
Review		
Say and Spell		
Arrange and Spell		
Complete and Spell		

Using SCVCR to Learn to Spell Music and Art Words

Look at the music and art words. Place a ✔ in front of two words you want to learn to spell.

| artist dancer ballet |
| texture conductor palette |
| portrait musician rhythm |

Write one word at the top of each column. Follow the steps in SCVCR to learn to spell each word. Use the prompts to help you remember what to do. In each box write what is needed or place a ✔ to show that you have completed the task.

	Word: _____	Word: _____
Say		
Say word		
Copy word		
See if correct		
Count		
# syllables		
Spell each syllable		
Visualize		
See word in mind		
Write word from memory		
Compare		
See if correct		
Repeat steps if incorrect		
Add to "My Personal Spelling List"		
Review		
Say and Spell		
Arrange and Spell		
Complete and Spell		

Using SCVCR to Learn to Spell Recreation Words

Look at the recreation words. Place a ✔ in front of two words you want to learn to spell.

| quarterback museum collect |
| antique pitcher forward |
| putter tackle soccer |

Write one word at the top of each column. Follow the steps in SCVCR to learn to spell each word. Use the prompts to help you remember what to do. In each box write what is needed or place a ✔ to show that you have completed the task.

Word: _____   Word: _____

Say

Say word		
Copy word		
See if correct		

Count

# syllables		
Spell each syllable		

Visualize

See word in mind		
Write word from memory		

Compare

See if correct		
Repeat steps if incorrect		
Add to "My Personal Spelling List"		

Review

Say and Spell		
Arrange and Spell		
Complete and Spell		

Using SCVCR to Learn to Spell Words You Choose

Choose two words you want to learn to spell. Write one word at the top of each column. Follow the steps in the SCVCR to learn to spell each word. Use the prompts to help you remember what to do. In each box write what is needed or place a ✔ to show that you have completed the task.

Word: _____ Word: _____

Say

Say word		
Copy word		
See if correct		

Count

# syllables		
Spell each syllable		

Visualize

See word in mind		
Write word from memory		

Compare

See if correct		
Repeat steps if incorrect		
Add to "My Personal Spelling List"		

Review

Say and Spell		
Arrange and Spell		
Complete and Spell		

Here are two words your teacher wants you to learn to spell. Write one word at the top of each column. Follow the steps in the SCVCR to learn to spell each word. Use the prompts to help you remember what to do. In each box write what is needed or place a ✔ to show that you have completed the task.

Word: _____   Word: _____

Say

Say word		
Copy word		
See if correct		

Count

# syllables		
Spell each syllable		

Visualize

See word in mind		
Write word from memory		

Compare

See if correct		
Repeat steps if incorrect		
Add to "My Personal Spelling List"		

Review

Say and Spell		
Arrange and Spell		
Complete and Spell		

1. For each letter of SCVCR, write the word the letter helps you remember.

    S = _____

    C = _____

    V = _____

    C = _____

    R = _____

2. Explain how SCVCR is used to learn to spell a word. Be sure to tell what you should do for each of the five steps.

    _____

    _____

    _____

    _____

    _____

3. Write the name and steps of one of the review routines.

    _____

    _____

    _____

    _____

    _____

Reflection How has learning the SCVCR spelling strategy made you a better student?

_____

_____

_____

ANSWER KEY FOR CHAPTER TWELVE

12-1 Responses will vary.

12-2 Recording page: No response required.

12-3 Demonstration page: No response required.

12-4 Students add their own review routines.

12-5 to 12-12 Words vary.

12-13 1. S=Say, C=Count, V=Visualize, C=Compare, R=Review. 2. Student responses should include the important ideas in the SCVCR steps. 3. Student responses should accurately provide the steps for any one of the three review routines.

Reflection Responses will vary but should reveal insights into how the student has become a better learner.

HOW TO ORDER AN UNLIMITED CD-ROM ASSESSMENT

The CD-Rom Assessment included with this book is a TRIAL VERSION that can be used with five students. An UNLIMITED VERSION that can be used with any number of students any number of times can be purchased from Mangrum-Strichart Learning Resources. To order or learn more:

Visit our website at: www.mangrum-strichart.com

or

Call our toll free number: 866-409-0585

Features of the Unlimited Assessment:

1. Can be administered to any number of students an UNLIMITED number of times.
2. Can be customized to assess any or all of the study skills and strategies taught in the book.
3. Can be self-administered by individual students in 15 to 20 minutes.
4. Provides a DIAGNOSTIC PROFILE for individualizing instruction.
5. Provides a NARRATIVE REPORT for communicating results to parents.
6. Provides a RECOMMENDATIONS AND INSTRUCTIONAL OBJECTIVES REPORT for IEP development
7. Can be administered multiple times to the same student to assess progress.
8. Is WIN or Mac ready.
9. Is network ready.

MANGRUM-STRICHART LEARNING RESOURCES

The Study Skills and Strategies Specialists

You should carefully read the following terms and conditions before opening this disk package.
Opening this disk package indicates your acceptance of these terms and conditions.
If you do **not** agree with them, you should promptly return the package unopened.

Allyn and Bacon provides this Program and License its use. You assume responsibility for the selection of the Program to achieve your intended results, and for the installation, use, and results obtained from the Program. This License extends only to use of the Program in the United States or countries in which the Program is marketed by duly authorized distributors.

License Grant

You hereby accept a nonexclusive, nontransferable, permanent License to install and use the Program on a single computer at any given time. You may copy the Program solely for backup or archival purposes in support of your use of the Program on the single computer. You may **not** modify, translate, disassemble, decompile, or reverse engineer the Program, in whole or in part.

Term

This License is effective until terminated. Allyn and Bacon reserves the right to terminate this License automatically if any provision of the License is violated. You may terminate the License at any time. To terminate this License, you must return the Program, including documentation, along with a written warranty stating that all copies of the Program in your possession have been returned or destroyed.

Limited Warranty

The Program is provided "As Is" without warranty of any kind, either express or implied, including, but **not** limited to, the implied warranties or merchantability and fitness for a particular purpose. The entire risk as to the quality and performance of the Program is with you. Should the Program prove defective, you (and **not** Allyn and Bacon or any authorized distributor) assume the entire cost of all necessary servicing, repair, or correction. No oral or written information or advice given by Allyn and Bacon, its dealers, distributors, or agents shall create a warranty or increase the scope of its warranty.

Some states do **not** allow the exclusion of implied warranty, so the above exclusion may **not** apply to you. This warranty gives you specific legal rights and you may also have other rights that vary from state to state.

Allyn and Bacon does **not** warrant that the functions contained in the Program will meet your requirements or that the operation of the Program will be uninterrupted or error free.

However, Allyn and Bacon warrants the disk(s) on which the Program is furnished to be free from defects in material and workmanship under normal use for a period of ninety (90) days from the date of delivery to you as evidenced by a copy of your receipt.

The Program should **not** be relied on as the sole basis to solve a problem whose incorrect solution could result in injury to a person or property. If the Program is

employed in such a manner, it is at the user's own risk and Allyn and Bacon explicitly disclaims all liability for such misuse.

Limitation of Remedies

Allyn and Bacon's entire liability and your exclusive remedy shall be:

1. The replacement of any disk **not** meeting Allyn and Bacon's "Limited Warranty" and that is returned to Allyn and Bacon or

2. If Allyn and Bacon is unable to deliver a replacement disk or cassette that is free of defects in materials or workmanship, you may terminate this Agreement by returning the Program.

In no event will Allyn and Bacon be liable to you for any damages, including any lost profits, lost savings, or other incidental or consequential damages arising out of the use or inability to use such Program even if Allyn and Bacon or an authorized distributor has been advised of the possibility of such damages of for any claim by any other party.

Some states do **not** allow the limitation or exclusion of liability for incidental or consequential damages, so the above limitation or exclusion may **not** apply to you.

General

You may **not** sublicense, assign, or transfer the License of the Program. Any attempt to sublicense, assign, or transfer any of the rights, duties, or obligations hereunder is void.

This Agreement will be governed by the laws of the Commonwealth of Massachusetts.

Should you have any questions concerning this Agreement, or any questions concerning technical support, you may contact Allyn and Bacon by writing to:

Allyn and Bacon
A Pearson Education Company
75 Arlington Street
Boston, MA 02116

You acknowledge that you have read this Agreement, understand it, and agree to be bound by its terms and conditions. You further agree that it is the complete and exclusive statement of the Agreement between us that supersedes any proposal or prior Agreement, oral or written, and any other communications between us relating to the subject matter of this Agreement.

Notice to Government End Users

The Program is provided with restricted rights. Use, duplication, or disclosure by the Government is subject to restrictions set forth in subdivison (b)(3)(iii) of The Rights in Technical Data and Computer Software Clause 252.227-7013.